Navigating the ELPS
in the Science Classroom

*Using the Standards to Improve
Instruction for English Language Learners*

John Seidlitz
Jennifer Jordan-Kaszuba

Seidlitz Education
P.O. Box 166827
Irving, TX 75016

© 2010 Sedilitz Education

ISBN 978-0-9822078-2-6

For related titles and support materials visit wwww.johnseidlitz.com.

Table of Contents

English Language Learners in Texas and the New Proficiency Standards ... 5

How to Use this Manual ... 6

Introduction (subsection a) ... 9

District Responsibilities (subsection b) ... 15

- *Understanding the ELPS Framework* ... 18
- *ELPS District Implementation Checklist* ... 20
- *ELPS Aligned Walk-Through Observation* ... 22

Cross-Curricular Student Expectations (subsection c) ... 25

- *ELPS Integration Plan for Teachers* ... 32
- *Seven Steps to Building a Language-Rich Interactive Classroom* ... 33
- *Language Objectives Aligned to Student Expectations* ... 34
- *ELPS Lesson Plan Template* ... 36
- *ELPS Lesson Plan Activity Guide* ... 40
- *Science Activities that Promote Language Development*
  - Conducting an Inquiry Based Experiment ... 41
  - Science Happens ... 44
  - Which Way Did It Go? A Walk Through the Nitrogen Cycle ... 45
  - Putting the Pieces Together: Connection Card Sort ... 52

- *Sentence Stems and Activities Aligned to Student Expectations* ... 59

Language Proficiency Level Descriptors (subsection d) ... 99

Guide to Terms and Activities ... 117

Bibliography ... 130

This page is intentionally left blank.

English Language Learners in Texas and the New Proficiency Standards

Research into what works for English Language Learners indicates that one of the keys to success is a consistent focus on content area language acquisition (Gibbons, P., 2002; Samway, K., 2006; Echevarria, Vogt, Short, 2008; Zweirs, J. 2008). This approach emphasizes the need to intentionally make content comprehensible while developing academic language skills for students acquiring English as a second language. It also requires academic language instruction be integrated into all areas of instruction so that all teachers of ELLs understand their role as a teacher of both content and language.

In 1998, the second language acquisition (ESL) standards were adopted as part of the Texas Essential Knowledge and Skills for Spanish Language Arts and English Language Arts. These standards included student expectations and descriptions of proficiency levels for reading, writing, listening, and speaking for students at various levels of language proficiency. Because these standards were only integrated into English and Spanish Language Arts, few content area teachers made use of them when planning instruction for English Language Learners.

In 2006, the Texas Education Agency assembled a group to review and revise the ESL standards. The result was the new English Language Proficiency Standards that went into effect in December of 2007. The standards describe the instruction that districts need to provide for English Language Learners so that they can successfully master both content area knowledge and academic language. Unlike the former ESL standards, the new standards clearly indicate that the ELPS are to be integrated into each subject of the required curriculum. The new ELPS contain a brief introduction into what kind of instruction is required for English Language Learners, an outline of district responsibilities, cross curricular student expectations, and language proficiency level descriptors.

Although integrating the ELPS into content areas will take time and effort for Texas educators, the new standards provide a unique opportunity to improve instruction for English Language Learners. The purpose of this manual is to provide resources and tools that will help make the process of implementation easier for administrators, specialists, and teachers who serve English Language Learners in classrooms across Texas.

How to Use this Manual

This manual is designed to help teachers, administrators and specialists use the ELPS (*http://www.tea.state.tx.us/rules/tac/chapter074/ch074a.html*) to improve instruction for English Language Learners. It is divided into four sections corresponding to the four sections of the English Language Proficiency Standards:

      (a)   Introduction
      (b)   District responsibilities
      (c)   Cross-curricular student expectations
      (d)   Language proficiency level descriptors

Each section begins with the text of the subsection of chapter 74.4 (TAC) that the tools and resources will address. This is followed by an assessment of current levels of understanding and implementation. The assessment is designed to guide administrators, educators and specialists through a process of deciding which tools and resources will best meet their current needs.   The assessment is followed by tools for understanding the meaning of the document as well as templates for implementing changes at the classroom, campus, and district levels in line with the new standards.

Section (a) addresses the introduction to the *English Language Proficiency Standards (2008).*   This section includes summaries of: the introduction (subsection a), district responsibilities (subsection b), student expectations (subsection c) and language proficiency level descriptors (subsection d). The summaries are followed by a handout listing reasons why the ELPS are significant to the instruction of English Language Learners in Texas.

Section (b) outlines district responsibilities discussed in the ELPS. The first set of tools is designed to help educators understand the ELPS framework for English proficiency.   They help clarify specific terms found in chapter 74.4. The terms ***communicated, sequenced,*** and ***scaffolded*** that describe ***linguistically accommodated instruction*** and the terms ***focused, targeted, and systematic*** that describe high quality second language acquisition instruction are discussed. The next set of tools includes an implementation checklist and a series of planning, observation, and coaching tools that can be used to meet the needs of teachers and administrators implementing ELPS at the classroom or campus level.

Section (c) addresses cross-curricular student expectations. The tools are designed to help educators integrate the ELPS into content area instruction. A quick guide to reading the new standards is included as well as specific lesson planning templates and sample lessons aligned to the ELPS. An ELPS Integration Plan for Teachers walks educators through a process for creating lesson plans that target academic language and concept development. Another tool outlines a seven step process for using the ELPS to create a language rich interactive classroom. The last tool in this section is a comprehensive guide for planning instruction using the ELPS that includes activities and suggested sentence stems that can be used with each of the standards.

Section (d) contains tools and resources for planning instruction based on students' language proficiency levels. A summary of each language level and specific strategies corresponding to each proficiency level as well as tools for differentiating instruction are provided. The section does not include tools for formal assessment of English Language Learners nor linguistic accommodations for English Language Learners taking the Linguistically Accommodated Testing (LAT). These can be found at the Texas Education Agency website: http://portals.tea.state.tx.us/page.aspx?id=568.

Guide to Terms and Activities: This section contains a description of each of the activities and strategies mentioned in the manual as well as references for further research on the activity.

This page is intentionally left blank.

Introduction

(subsection a)

Chapter 74. Curriculum Requirements: Subchapter A. Required Curriculum

§74.4. English Language Proficiency Standards
http://www.tea.state.tx.us/rules/tac/chapter074/ch074a.html.

(a) Introduction.

(1) The English Language Proficiency Standards in this section outline English language proficiency level descriptors and student expectations for English Language Learners (ELLs). School districts shall implement this section as an integral part of each subject in the required curriculum. The English Language Proficiency Standards are to be published along with the Texas Essential Knowledge and Skills (TEKS) for each subject in the required curriculum.

(2) In order for ELLs to be successful, they must acquire both social and academic language proficiency in English. Social language proficiency in English consists of the English needed for daily social interactions. Academic language proficiency consists of the English needed to think critically, understand and learn new concepts, process complex academic material, and interact and communicate in English academic settings.

(3) Classroom instruction that effectively integrates second language acquisition with quality content area instruction ensures that ELLs acquire social and academic language proficiency in English, learn the knowledge and skills in the TEKS, and reach their full academic potential.

(4) Effective instruction in second language acquisition involves giving ELLs opportunities to listen, speak, read, and write at their current levels of English development while gradually increasing the linguistic complexity of the English they read and hear, and are expected to speak and write.

(5) The cross-curricular second language acquisition skills in subsection (c) of this section apply to ELLs in Kindergarten-Grade 12.

(6) The English Language Proficiency Levels of beginning, intermediate, advanced, and advanced high are not grade-specific. ELLs may exhibit different proficiency levels within the language domains of listening, speaking, reading, and writing. The proficiency level descriptors outlined in subsection (d) of this section show the progression of second language acquisition from one proficiency level to the next and serve as a road map to help content area teachers instruct ELLs commensurate with students' linguistic needs.

ELPS Awareness Self-Assessment

Rate the current level of awareness of the English Language Proficiency Standards at your district or campus.

A: Always
M: Mostly

S: Sometimes
N: Never

Indicator	A	M	S	N	Comments/Questions
Teachers of ELLs are aware of the unique needs of ELLs to acquire social language skills for social interaction.					
Teachers of ELLs are aware of the unique needs of ELLs to acquire academic language necessary for academic tasks.					
Teachers of ELLs are aware of the need to integrate language and content instruction to ensure that ELLs acquire social and academic English.					
Teachers of ELLs receive staff development on the unique needs of ELLs to acquire social and academic English.					
ELLs are assessed for their language proficiency level upon entry into the district.					
Teachers of ELLs are aware of the language levels of their students on the initial district assessment and on the TELPAS.					
Administrators, teachers, and specialists are aware of the need to integrate the cross-curricular student expectations of the ELPS into content area instruction.					

Summaries of ELPS*
Introduction, District Responsibilities, and Student Expectations
(subsection a,b,c)

Introduction	District Responsibilities
a1: This part states the required curriculum for each subject including **proficiency standards** and **level descriptors** a2: ELLs need social and academic English language proficiency to be successful a3: Instruction must integrate **social and academic English** in content areas a4: ELLs must read, write, listen, and speak in increasing complexity a5: Student Expectations of ELPS apply to K-12 students a6: Level descriptors are not grade specific and serve as a road map.	b1: Identify students' proficiency levels using proficiency level descriptors b2: Provide **linguistically accommodated** content instruction (<u>communicated</u>, <u>sequenced</u>, <u>scaffolded</u>) b3: Provide linguistically accommodated content-based language instruction b4: Focused, targeted, and systematic language instruction for beginning and intermediate ELLs (Grade 3 or higher)

Learning Strategies	
c1A: Use prior knowledge to learn new language c1B: Monitor language with self-corrective techniques c1C: Use techniques to learn new vocabulary c1D: Speak using learning strategies	c1E: Use and reuse new basic and academic language to internalize language c1F: Use accessible language to learn new language c1G: Distinguish formal and informal English c1H: Expand repertoire of language learning strategies

Listening	Speaking
c2A: Distinguish sound and intonation c2B: Recognize English sound system in new vocabulary c2C: Learn new language heard in classroom interactions and instruction c2D: Monitor understanding and seek clarification c2E: Use visual, contextual linguistic support to confirm and enhance understanding c2F: Derive meaning from a variety of media c2G: Understand general meaning, main points, and details c2H: Understand implicit ideas and information c2I: Demonstrate listening comprehension	c3A: Practice using English sound system in new vocabulary c3B: Use new vocabulary in stories, descriptions, and classroom communication c3C: Speak using a variety of sentence structures c3D: Speak using grade level content area vocabulary in context c3E: Share in cooperative groups c3F: Ask and give information using high-frequency and content area vocabulary c3G: Express opinions, ideas, and feelings c3H: Narrate, describe, and explain c3I: Adapt spoken language for formal and informal purposes c3J: Respond orally to information from a variety of media sources

Reading	Writing
c4A: Learn relationships of sounds and letters in English c4B: Recognize directionality of English text c4C: Develop sight vocabulary and language structures c4D: Use prereading supports c4E: Read linguistically accommodated content area materials c4F: Use visual and contextual supports to read text c4G: Show comprehension of English text individually and in groups c4H: Read silently with comprehension c4I: Show comprehension through basic reading skills c4J: Show comprehension through inferential skills c4K: Show comprehension through analytical skills	c5A: Learn relationships between sounds and letters when writing c5B: Write using newly acquired vocabulary c5C: Spell familiar English words c5D: Edit writing c5E: Employ complex grammatical structures c5F: Write using variety of sentence structures and words c5G: Narrate, describe, and explain in writing

* These summaries must be used in conjunction with cross-curricular student expectations when planning instruction.

Summaries of ELPS: Proficiency Level Descriptors*
(subsection d)

Level	Listening (d1: k-12) The student comprehends...	Speaking (d2: k-12) The student speaks...	Reading (d4: 2-12) The student reads...	Writing (d6: 2-12) The student writes...
Beginning (A)	1A(i) few simple conversations with linguistic support 1A(ii) modified conversation 1A(iii) few words, does not seek clarification, watches others for cues	2A(i) using single words and short phrases with practiced material; tends to give up on attempts 2A(ii) using limited bank of key vocabulary 2A(iii) with recently practiced familiar material 2A(iv) with frequent errors that hinder communication 2A(v) with pronunciation that inhibits communication	4A(i) little except recently practiced terms, environmental print, high frequency words, concrete words represented by pictures 4A(ii) slowly, word by word 4A(iii) with very limited sense of English structure 4A(iv) with comprehension of practiced, familiar text 4A(v) with need for visuals and prior knowledge 4A(vi) modified and adapted text	6A(i) with little ability to use English 6A(ii) without focus and coherence, conventions, organization, voice 6A(iii) labels, lists, and copies of printed text and high-frequency words/phrases, short and simple, practiced sentences primarily in present tense with frequent errors that hinder or prevent understanding
Intermediate (B)	1B(i) unfamiliar language with linguistic supports and adaptations 1B(ii) unmodified conversation with key words and phrases 1B(iii) with requests for clarification by asking speaker to repeat, slow down, or rephrase speech	2B(i) with simple messages and hesitation to think about meaning 2B(ii) using basic vocabulary 2B(iii) with simple sentence structures and present tense 2B(iv) with errors that inhibit unfamiliar communication 2B(v) with pronunciation generally understood by those familiar with English Language Learners	4B(i) wider range of topics: and everyday academic language 4B(ii) slowly and rereads 4B(iii) basic language structures 4B(iv) simple sentences with visual cues, pretaught vocabulary and interaction 4B(v) grade-level texts with difficulty 4B(vi) at high level with linguistic accommodation	6B(i) with limited ability to use English in content area writing 6B(ii) best on topics that are highly familiar with simple English 6B(iii) with simple oral tone in messages, high-frequency vocabulary, loosely connected text, repetition of ideas, mostly in the present tense, undetailed descriptions, and frequent errors
Advanced (C)	1C(i) with some processing time, visuals, verbal cues, and gestures; for unfamiliar conversations 1C(ii) most unmodified interaction 1C(iii) with occasional requests for the speaker to slow down, repeat, rephrase, and clarify meaning	2C(i) in conversations with some pauses to restate, repeat, and clarify 2C(ii) using content-based and abstract terms on familiar topics 2C(iii) with past, present, and future 2C(iv) using complex sentences and grammar with some errors 2C(v) with pronunciation usually understood by most	4C(i) abstract grade appropriate text 4C(ii) longer phrases and familiar sentences appropriately 4C(iii) while developing the ability to construct meaning from text 4C(iv) at high comprehension level with linguistic support for unfamiliar topics and to clarify meaning	6C(i) grade appropriate ideas with second language support 6C(ii) with extra need for second language support when topics are technical and abstract 6C(iii) with a grasp of basic English usage and some understanding of complex usage with emerging grade-appropriate vocabulary and a more academic tone
Advanced High (D)	1D(i) longer discussions on unfamiliar topics 1D(ii) spoken information nearly comparable to native speaker 1D(iii) with few requests for speaker to slow down, repeat, or rephrase	2D(i) in extended discussions with few pauses 2D(ii) using abstract content-based vocabulary except low frequency terms; using idioms 2D(iii) with grammar nearly comparable to native speaker 2D(iv) with few errors blocking communication 2D(v) occasional mispronunciation	4D(i) nearly comparable to native speakers 4D(ii) grade appropriate familiar text appropriately 4D(iii) while constructing meaning at near native ability level 4D(iv) with high level comprehension with minimal linguistic support	6D(i) grade appropriate content area ideas with little need for linguistic support 6D(ii) develop and demonstrate grade appropriate writing 6D (iii) nearly comparable to native speakers with clarity and precision, with occasional difficulties with naturalness of language.

*These summaries are not appropriate to use in formally identifying student proficiency levels for TELPAS. TELPAS assessment and training materials are provided by the Texas Education Agency Student Assessment Division: http://www.tea.state.tx.us/index3.aspx?id=3300&menu_id3=793

Why the ELPS?

1. English Language Learners benefit from content area instruction that is accommodated to their need for comprehensible input (Krashen, 1983; Echevarria, Vogt, and Short, 2008).

2. English Language Learners benefit from academic language instruction integrated into content area instruction (Crandall, 1987; Snow et. al. 1989).

3. English Language Learners benefit from programs that hold high expectations for students for academic success (Collier, 1992; Lucas et al, 1990, Samway & McKeon 2007).

4. Language Proficiency Standards provide a common framework for integrating language and content instruction for English Language Learners (Short, 2000).

District Responsibilities

(subsection b)

§74.4. English Language Proficiency Standards
http://www.tea.state.tx.us/rules/tac/chapter074/ch074a.html.

(b) School district responsibilities. In fulfilling the requirements of this section, school districts shall:

(1) identify the student's English language proficiency levels in the domains of listening, speaking, reading, and writing in accordance with the proficiency level descriptors for the beginning, intermediate, advanced, and advanced high levels delineated in subsection (d) of this section;

(2) provide instruction in the knowledge and skills of the foundation and enrichment curriculum in a manner that is linguistically accommodated (communicated, sequenced, and scaffolded) commensurate with the student's levels of English language proficiency to ensure that the student learns the knowledge and skills in the required curriculum;

(3) provide content-based instruction including the cross-curricular second language acquisition essential knowledge and skills in subsection (c) of this section in a manner that is linguistically accommodated to help the student acquire English language proficiency; and

(4) provide intensive and ongoing foundational second language acquisition instruction to ELLs in Grade 3 or higher who are at the beginning or intermediate level of English language proficiency in listening, speaking, reading, and/or writing as determined by the state's English language proficiency assessment system. These ELLs require focused, targeted, and systematic second language acquisition instruction to provide them with the foundation of English language vocabulary, grammar, syntax, and English mechanics necessary to support content-based instruction and accelerated learning of English.

ELPS Implementation Self-Assessment

Rate the current level of implementation of the English Language Proficiency Standards at your district or campus.

A: Always   S: Sometimes
M: Mostly   N: Never

Understanding the ELPS Framework: (1)

Indicator	A	M	S	N	Comments/Questions
Teachers of ELLs receive sufficient training on how to provide ELLs instruction in social and academic English.					
Teachers of ELLs receive sufficient training on how to differentiate instruction based on the language levels of English Language Learners.					
Teachers of ELLs integrate language and content area instruction in their lesson plans.					
Teachers of ELLs provide linguistically accommodated instruction to meet the language proficiency levels of their English Language Learners.					
ELLs have opportunities to read and write in academic English during content area instruction.					
ELLs have opportunities to listen and speak using academic English during content area instruction.					
The cross-curricular student expectations are being integrated into existing curriculum frameworks.					
The cross-curricular student expectations are being integrated into content area lesson plans.					

Understanding the ELPS Framework : (1)
Linguistically Accommodated Instruction

Curriculum for ELLs must be:	What is it?	What are some examples?
Communicated	Comprehensible input is used to convey the meaning of key concepts to students. (Krashen, 1983)	• Visuals, TPR (Total Physical Response) and other techniques to communicate key concepts • Clear explanation of academic tasks • Speech appropriate for language level • Use of Native Language Resources (Echevarria, Vogt, Short, 2008)
Sequenced	Instruction is differentiated to align with the progression of students' language development level. (Hill & Flynn, 2006)	• Differentiating language and content instruction • Targeted use of supplementary materials and resources • Pre-teaching social and academic vocabulary necessary for interaction and classroom tasks (Hill & Flynn, 2006)
Scaffolded	ELLs receive structured support that leads to independent acquisition of language and content knowledge. (Echevarria, Vogt, Short, 2008)	• **Oral scaffolding:** recasting, paraphrasing, wait time, etc. • **Procedural scaffolding:** moving from whole class, to group, to individual tasks. • **Instructional scaffolding:** providing concrete structures such as sentence and paragraph frames, patterns, and models. (Echevarria, Vogt, & Short, 2008)

Understanding the ELPS Framework: (2)
Foundations of Second Language Acquisition Instruction
for Beginning and Intermediate ELLs Grades 3-12

"Make sure the system for second language acquisition instruction focuses on the target."

Second language acquisition instruction must be:	What is it?	What are some examples?
Focused	**Concentrated effort centered on student acquisition** of vocabulary, grammar, syntax, and English mechanics necessary to support content-based instruction and accelerated learning of English.	• Explicit instruction in English vocabulary and language structures • Lesson plans include cross-curricular student expectations from the ELPS. • Use of sentence structures of increasing complexity in vocabulary, grammar, and syntax
Targeted	**Specific goals and objectives** align with vocabulary, grammar, syntax, and English mechanics necessary to support content-based instruction and accelerated learning of English.	• Content objectives for ELLs align with the TEKS • Language objectives for ELLs align with ELPS and language skills necessary for TEKS • Formal and informal assessments align with content and language assessments
Systematic	**Well-organized structure** in place to ensure students acquire vocabulary, grammar, syntax, and English mechanics necessary to support content-based instruction and accelerated learning of English.	• ELPS integrated into district curriculum frameworks • **Comprehensive plan for students in grades 3-12 at beginner or intermediate** level for integrating language and content instruction • Comprehensive plan for assessing the implementation of focused, targeted instruction for beginner and intermediate students in grades 3-12 • Periodic review of progress of ELLs through formal and informal assessment

ELPS District Implementation Checklist

Goal	We will have met this goal when...	Steps	Person(s) Responsible	Dates/Deadlines
Administrators and specialists integrate ELPS into ongoing professional development and evaluation.				
Staff understands the importance of TELPAS and other formal assessments to identify language levels of ELLs.				
Staff understands the need for ELLs to develop social and academic English.				
Staff understands methods for providing linguistically accommodated instruction for ELLs.				
Staff understands cross-curricular student expectations.				
Staff develops a plan for systematic academic language development for ELLs.				
Teachers include ELPS in lesson plans in core content areas.				

Two Key Questions for Assessing Quality Instruction for ELLs

Do English Language Learners understand the key content concepts (aligned to *TEKS*)?	Are English Language Learners developing their ability to read, write, listen, and speak in academic English about content concepts (*in ways described in the ELPS*)?

ELPS Aligned Walk-Through Observation

Observer: Class:

Teacher: Date:

Indicator	Comments/Questions
☐ Content and language objectives posted	
☐ Evidence of explicit vocabulary instruction	
☐ Evidence of a variety of techniques used to make content comprehensible	
☐ Evidence of reading and writing in academic English	
☐ Evidence of student/student interaction focusing on lesson concepts	
☐ Specific instructional interventions for ELLs appropriate to students' language levels (sentence stems, native language resources, word banks, low risk environment for language production, etc.)	

ELPS Aligned Lesson Observation

Observer: Class:

Teacher: Date:

Indicator	Comments/Questions
☐ Teacher posts and explains clearly defined content objectives aligned to the TEKS for ELLs.	
☐ Teacher posts and explains clearly defined language objectives aligned to the ELPS for ELLs.	
☐ Teacher clearly communicates key concepts, words, phrases, and directions for instructional tasks to ELLs (using visuals, gestures, native language resources, etc. as needed).	
☐ Teacher differentiates instruction (alters instruction, language demands and assessment) to align with the students' language development level.	
☐ Teacher provides verbal and procedural scaffolding for ELLs (sentence stems, modeling, instructional strategies, etc.).	
☐ Teacher provides opportunities for students to read and write using academic English.	
☐ Teacher provides opportunities for ELLs to listen and speak using academic and social English.	
☐ ELLs demonstrate understanding of content and language objectives.	

ELPS Aligned Lesson Observation Coaching Tool

Observer: Class:

Teacher: Date:

Indicator	Comments/Questions
☐ Teacher posts and explains clearly defined content objectives aligned to the TEKS for ELLs.	• Are the objectives posted? • Do ELLs understand the objectives? • Are the objectives aligned with the TEKS? • Does the lesson align with the objectives?
☐ Teacher posts and explains clearly defined language objectives aligned to the ELPS for ELLs.	• Are the objectives posted? • Do ELLs understand the objectives? • Are the objectives aligned with the ELPS? • Does the lesson align with the objectives?
☐ Teacher clearly communicates key concepts, words, phrases and directions for instructional tasks to English Language Learners (*using visuals, gestures, native language resources, etc. as needed*).	• Do ELLs understand the key concepts? • Does the teacher explicitly teach key concept area vocabulary? • Does the teacher teach ELLs specific words and phrases necessary for instructional tasks? • Do ELLs show a clear understanding of instructional tasks?
☐ Teacher differentiates instruction (*alters instruction, language demands, and assessment*) to align with the students' language development level.	• Is the teacher aware of the students' language levels? • Are instructions, assignments, and assessments appropriate for the students' level of language development?
☐ Teacher provides verbal and procedural scaffolding for ELLs. (*sentence stems, modeling, instruction in strategies etc.*)	• Does the teacher provide models, examples, and structures that enable ELLs to work toward independence? • Do ELLs use specific strategies when they need clarification about content or language?
☐ Teacher provides opportunities for students to read and write using academic English.	• Do ELLs read academic English during the lesson? • Do ELLs write during the lesson? • Are ELLs supported in finding ways to enable them to read and write during the lesson?
☐ Teacher provides opportunities for ELLs to listen and speak using academic and social English.	• Do ELLs listen and speak using social English? • Do ELLs use content area vocabulary during classroom interactions? • Do ELLs use academic English structures during classroom interactions?
☐ ELLs demonstrate understanding of content and language objectives.	• Are ELLs assessed throughout the lesson for understanding of content and language?

Cross-Curricular
Student Expectations

(subsection c)

§74.4. English Language Proficiency Standards
http://www.tea.state.tx.us/rules/tac/chapter074/ch074a.html.

(c) Cross-curricular Student Expectations

(1) Cross-curricular second language acquisition/learning strategies. The ELL uses language learning strategies to develop an awareness of his or her own learning processes in all content areas. In order for the ELL to meet grade-level learning expectations across the foundation and enrichment curriculum, all instruction delivered in English must be linguistically accommodated (communicated, sequenced, and scaffolded) commensurate with the student's level of English language proficiency. The student is expected to:

(A) use prior knowledge and experiences to understand meanings in English;

(B) monitor oral and written language production and employ self-corrective techniques or other resources;

(C) use strategic learning techniques such as concept mapping, drawing, memorizing, comparing, contrasting, and reviewing to acquire basic and grade-level vocabulary;

(D) speak using learning strategies such as requesting assistance, employing non-verbal cues, and using synonyms and circumlocution (conveying ideas by defining or describing when exact English words are not known);

(E) internalize new basic and academic language by using and reusing it in meaningful ways in speaking and writing activities that build concept and language attainment;

(F) use accessible language and learn new and essential language in the process;

(G) demonstrate an increasing ability to distinguish between formal and informal English and an increasing knowledge of when to use each one commensurate with grade-level learning expectations; and

(H) develop and expand repertoire of learning strategies such as reasoning inductively or deductively, looking for patterns in language, and analyzing sayings and expressions commensurate with grade-level learning expectations.

(2) Cross-curricular second language acquisition/listening. The ELL listens to a variety of speakers including teachers, peers, and electronic media to gain an increasing level of comprehension of newly acquired language in all content areas. ELLs may be at the beginning, intermediate, advanced, or advanced high stage of English language acquisition in listening. In order for the ELL to meet grade-level learning expectations across the foundation and enrichment curriculum, all instruction delivered in English must be linguistically accommodated (communicated, sequenced, and scaffolded) commensurate with the student's level of English language proficiency. The student is expected to:

(A) distinguish sounds and intonation patterns of English with increasing ease;

(B) recognize elements of the English sound system in newly acquired vocabulary such as long and short vowels, silent letters, and consonant clusters;

(C) learn new language structures, expressions, and basic and academic vocabulary heard during classroom instruction and interactions;

(D) monitor understanding of spoken language during classroom instruction and interactions and seek clarification as needed;

(E) use visual, contextual, and linguistic support to enhance and confirm understanding of increasingly complex and elaborated spoken language;

(F) listen to and derive meaning from a variety of media such as audio tape, video, DVD, and CD ROM to build and reinforce concept and language attainment;

(G) understand the general meaning, main points, and important details of spoken language ranging from situations in which topics, language, and contexts are familiar to unfamiliar;

(H) understand implicit ideas and information in increasingly complex spoken language commensurate with grade-level learning expectations; and

(I) demonstrate listening comprehension of increasingly complex spoken English by following directions, retelling or summarizing spoken messages, responding to questions and requests, collaborating with peers, and taking notes commensurate with content and grade-level needs.

(3) Cross-curricular second language acquisition/speaking. The ELL speaks in a variety of modes for a variety of purposes with an awareness of different language registers (formal/informal) using vocabulary with increasing fluency and accuracy in language arts and all content areas. ELLs may be at the beginning, intermediate, advanced, or advanced high stage of English language acquisition in speaking. In order for the ELL to meet grade-level learning expectations across the foundation and enrichment curriculum, all instruction delivered in English must be linguistically accommodated (communicated, sequenced, and scaffolded) commensurate with the student's level of English language proficiency. The student is expected to:

(A) practice producing sounds of newly acquired vocabulary such as long and short vowels, silent letters, and consonant clusters to pronounce English words in a manner that is increasingly comprehensible;

(B) expand and internalize initial English vocabulary by learning and using high-frequency English words necessary for identifying and describing people, places, and objects, by retelling simple stories and basic information represented or supported by pictures, and by learning and using routine language needed for classroom communication;

(C) speak using a variety of grammatical structures, sentence lengths, sentence types, and connecting words with increasing accuracy and ease as more English is acquired;

(D) speak using grade-level content area vocabulary in context to internalize new English words and build academic language proficiency;

(E) share information in cooperative learning interactions;

(F) ask and give information ranging from using a very limited bank of high-frequency, high-need, concrete vocabulary, including key words and expressions needed for basic communication in academic and social contexts, to using abstract and content-based vocabulary during extended speaking assignments;

(G) express opinions, ideas, and feelings ranging from communicating single words and short phrases to participating in extended discussions on a variety of social and grade-appropriate academic topics;

(H) narrate, describe, and explain with increasing specificity and detail as more English is acquired;

(I) adapt spoken language appropriately for formal and informal purposes; and

(J) respond orally to information presented in a wide variety of print, electronic, audio, and visual media to build and reinforce concept and language attainment.

(4) Cross-curricular second language acquisition/reading. The ELL reads a variety of texts for a variety of purposes with an increasing level of comprehension in all content areas. ELLs may be at the beginning, intermediate, advanced, or advanced high stage of English language acquisition in reading. In order for the ELL to meet grade-level learning expectations across the foundation and enrichment curriculum, all instruction delivered in English must be linguistically accommodated (communicated, sequenced, and scaffolded) commensurate with the student's level of English language proficiency. For Kindergarten and Grade 1, certain of these student expectations apply to text read aloud for students not yet at the stage of decoding written text. The student is expected to:

(A) learn relationships between sounds and letters of the English language and decode (sound out) words using a combination of skills such as recognizing sound-letter relationships and identifying cognates, affixes, roots, and base words;

(B) recognize directionality of English reading such as left to right and top to bottom;

(C) develop basic sight vocabulary, derive meaning of environmental print, and comprehend English vocabulary and language structures used routinely in written classroom materials;

(D) use prereading supports such as graphic organizers, illustrations, and pretaught topic-related vocabulary and other prereading activities to enhance comprehension of written text;

(E) read linguistically accommodated content area material with a decreasing need for linguistic accommodations as more English is learned;

(F) use visual and contextual support and support from peers and teachers to read grade-appropriate content area text, to enhance and confirm understanding, to develop vocabulary, to grasp language structures, and to tap background knowledge needed to comprehend increasingly challenging language;

(G) demonstrate comprehension of increasingly complex English by participating in shared reading, retelling or summarizing material, responding to questions, and taking notes commensurate with content area and grade level needs;

(H) read silently with increasing ease and comprehension for longer periods;

(I) demonstrate English comprehension and expand reading skills by employing basic reading skills such as demonstrating understanding of supporting ideas and details in text and graphic sources, summarizing text, and distinguishing main ideas from details commensurate with content area needs;

(J) demonstrate English comprehension and expand reading skills by employing inferential skills such as predicting, making connections between ideas, drawing inferences and conclusions from text and graphic sources, and finding supporting text evidence commensurate with content area needs; and

(K) demonstrate English comprehension and expand reading skills by employing analytical skills such as evaluating written information and performing critical analyses commensurate with content area and grade-level needs.

(5) Cross-curricular second language acquisition/writing. The ELL writes in a variety of forms with increasing accuracy to effectively address a specific purpose and audience in all content areas. ELLs may be at the beginning, intermediate, advanced, or advanced high stage of English language acquisition in writing. In order for the ELL to meet grade-level learning expectations across foundation

and enrichment curriculum, all instruction delivered in English must be linguistically accommodated (communicated, sequenced, and scaffolded) commensurate with the student's level of English language proficiency. For Kindergarten and Grade 1, certain of these student expectations do not apply until the student has reached the stage of generating original written text using a standard writing system. The student is expected to:

(A) learn relationships between sounds and letters of the English language to represent sounds when writing in English;

(B) write using newly acquired basic vocabulary and content-based grade-level vocabulary;

(C) spell familiar English words with increasing accuracy, and employ English spelling patterns and rules with increasing accuracy as more English is acquired;

(D) edit writing for standard grammar and usage, including subject-verb agreement, pronoun agreement, and appropriate verb tenses commensurate with grade-level expectations as more English is acquired;

(E) employ increasingly complex grammatical structures in content area writing commensurate with grade-level expectations, such as:

(i) using correct verbs, tenses, and pronouns/antecedents;

(ii) using possessive case (apostrophe s) correctly; and

(iii) using negatives and contractions correctly;

(F) write using a variety of grade-appropriate sentence lengths, patterns, and connecting words to combine phrases, clauses, and sentences in increasingly accurate ways as more English is acquired; and

(G) narrate, describe, and explain with increasing specificity and detail to fulfill content area writing needs as more English is acquired.

ELPS Integration into Lesson Planning: Self-Assessment

Rate the current level of integration of the English Language Proficiency Standards in your lessons.

A: Always

M: Mostly

S: Sometimes

N: Never

Indicator	A	M	S	N	Comments/Questions
I am aware of my district and school's program goals for ELLs.					
I am aware of specific instructional strategies to support ELLs in attaining English language proficiency.					
Students have opportunities to interact socially in my classroom.					
Students interact using academic English about key concepts in my classroom.					
Students read and write using academic English in my classroom.					
I set language objectives for my students.					
I have integrated the ELPS student expectations into my lessons.					
English Language Learners have opportunities to build vocabulary and concept knowledge.					

How to Read the Cross-Curricular Student Expectations

Cross-curricular student expectations are organized into five categories for second language acquisition:

1. learning strategies
2. listening
3. speaking
4. reading
5. writing

The knowledge and skills statement describes the intentions of the student expectations included in this section.

Each student expectation is listed individually by letter. These expectations can be used for creating curriculum frameworks, creating and documenting lesson plans, and writing language objectives for English Language Learners.

Note that some student expectations do not apply for students at early levels of literacy.

5) Cross-curricular second language acquisition/writing. *The ELL writes in a variety of forms with increasing accuracy to effectively address a specific purpose and audience in all content areas. ELLs may be at the beginning, intermediate, advanced, or advanced high stage of English language acquisition in writing. In order for the ELL to meet grade-level learning expectations across foundation and enrichment curriculum, all instruction delivered in English must be linguistically accommodated (communicated, sequenced, and scaffolded) commensurate with the student's level of English language proficiency.* **For Kindergarten and Grade 1, certain of these student expectations do not apply until the student has reached the stage of generating original written text using a standard writing system.** *The student is expected to:*

(A) learn relationships between sounds and letters of the English language to represent sounds when writing in English;

(B) write using newly acquired basic vocabulary and content-based grade-level vocabulary;

(C) spell familiar English words with increasing accuracy, and employ English spelling patterns and rules with increasing accuracy as more English is acquired;

(D) edit writing for standard grammar and usage, including subject-verb agreement, pronoun agreement, and appropriate verb tenses commensurate with grade-level expectations as more English is acquired

ELPS Integration Plan for Teachers

1. Identify the language proficiency levels of all ELLs.

2. Identify appropriate linguistic accommodations and strategies for differentiating instruction.

3. Take steps to build a language-rich interactive classroom.

4. Identify cross-curricular student expectations of the ELPS (subsection c) that could be integrated as language objectives into existing content area instruction.

5. Create focused lesson plans that target academic language and concept development.

Seven Steps to Building a Language-Rich Interactive Classroom

1.	Teach students language and strategies to use when they don't know what to say.	1B Monitor language with self-corrective techniques 1D Speak using learning strategies 1F Use accessible language to learn new language 1H Expand repertoire of learning strategies to acquire new language 2D Monitor understanding and seek clarification 2E Use linguistic support to confirm and enhance understanding
2.	Encourage students to speak in complete sentences.	1G Distinguish formal and informal English 3A Practice speaking using English sound system in new vocabulary 3C Speak using a variety of sentence structures 3D Speak using grade level vocabulary in context 3F Speak using common and content area vocabulary 3I Use oral language for formal and informal purposes
3.	Randomize and rotate who is called on so students of all language levels can participate.	1G Distinguish formal and informal English 3A Practice speaking using English sound system in new vocabulary 3C Speak using a variety of sentence structures 3D Speak using grade level vocabulary in context 3F Speak using common and content area vocabulary 3I Use oral language for formal and informal purposes
4.	Use response signals for students to monitor their own comprehension.	1B Monitor language with self-corrective techniques 2D Monitor understanding and seek clarification 2E Use linguistic support to confirm and enhance understanding 2I Demonstrate listening comprehension
5.	Use visuals and a focus on vocabulary to build background.	1A Use prior knowledge to learn new language 1C Use techniques to learn new vocabulary 2A Distinguish sound and intonation 2B Recognize English sound system in new vocabulary 2F Derive meaning from a variety of media 3J Respond orally to a variety of media sources 4A Learn relationships of sounds and letters in English 4C Develop sight vocabulary and language structures 5C Spell familiar English words
6.	Have students participate in structured reading activities.	4B Recognize directionality of English text 4D Use pre-reading supports 4E Read linguistically accommodated materials 4F Use visual and contextual supports to read text 4G Show comprehension of English text individually and in groups 4H Read silently with comprehension 4I Show comprehension through basic reading skills 4J Show comprehension through inferential skills 4K Show comprehension through analytical skills
7.	Have students participate in structured conversation and writing activities.	<div align="center">**Conversation**</div>1E Use and reuse basic and academic language 2C Learn language heard in interactions and instruction 2H Understand implicit ideas and information 2G Understand general meaning, main points, and details of spoken language 3B Use new vocabulary in stories, descriptions, and classroom communication 3G Orally express opinions ideas and feelings 3E Share in cooperative groups 3H Orally narrate, describe, and explain <div align="center">**Writing**</div>5A Learn relationships between sounds and letters when writing 5B Write using newly acquired vocabulary 5D Edit writing 5E Employ complex grammatical structures 5F Write using variety of sentence structures and words 5G Narrate, describe, and explain in writing

Language Objectives Aligned to Cross-Curricular Student Expectations
(subsection c)

Learning Strategies

1A: Use what they know about ___ to predict the meaning of ...
1B: Check how well they are able to say ...
1C: Use ___ to learn new vocabulary about...
1D: Use strategies such as ___ to discuss...
1E: Use and reuse the words/phrases ___ in a discussion/writing activity about...
1F: Use the phrase ___ to learn the meaning of ...
1G: Use formal/informal English to describe...
1H: Use strategies such as ___ to learn the meaning of.

Listening

2A: Recognize correct pronunciation of ....
2B: Recognize sounds used in the words ...
2C: Identify words and phrases heard in a discussion about ...
2D: Check for understanding by ..../Seek help by ...
2E: Use supports such as ___ to enhance understanding of ...
2F: Use __ (media source) to learn/review ....
2G: Describe general meaning, main points, and details heard in ...
2H: Identify implicit ideas and information heard in ...
2I: Demonstrate listening comprehension by...

Speaking

3A: Pronounce the words ___ correctly.
3B: Use new vocabulary about ___ in stories, pictures, descriptions, and/or classroom communication ...
3C: Speak using a variety of types of sentence stems about ...
3D: Speak using the words___ about...
3E: Share in cooperative groups about ...
3F: Ask and give information using the words...
3G: Express opinions, ideas, and feelings about ___ using the words/phrases...
3H: Narrate, describe, and explain ....
3I: Use formal/informal English to say ...
3J: Respond orally to information from a variety of media sources about...

Reading

4A: Identify relationships between sounds and letters by...
4B: Recognize directionality of English text.
4C: Recognize the words/phrases....
4D: Use prereading supports such as___ to understand ...
4E: Read materials about ___ with support of simplified text/visuals/word banks as needed.
4F: Use visual and contextual supports to read ...
4G: Show comprehension of English text about ...
4H: Demonstrate comprehension of text read silently by...
4I: Show comprehension of text about ___ through basic reading skills such as ...
4J: Show comprehension of text/graphic sources about ___ through inferential skills such as ...
4K: Show comprehension of text about ___ through analytical skills such as ...

Writing

5A: Learn relationships between sounds and letters when writing about ...
5B: Write using newly acquired vocabulary about...
5C: Spell English words such as ...
5D: Edit writing about ...
5E: Use simple and complex sentences to write about ..
5F: Write using a variety of sentence frames and selected vocabulary about ...
5G: Narrate, describe, and explain in writing about ...

Examples of Content and Language Objectives Aligned to the Science TEKS and Cross-Curricular Student Expectations

(subsection c)

TEKS	Content Objective	ELPS	Language Objective
Elementary			
K.9A	The learner will differentiate between living and nonliving things.	1C	The learner will use a card sort to categorize pictures as living or nonliving things.
1.5A	I will classify objects by what I can observe such as size, heaviness, shape, color, and texture.	1C	I can use Vocabulary Alive to learn new vocabulary to describe objects.
2.8A	We will record and graph weather information to see if there are patterns.	2F	We will listen to weather reports to obtain the daily weather information.
3.7C	The student will identify and compare different landforms, including mountains, hills, valleys, and plains.	3A	The student will pronounce the words landforms, mountains, hills, valley, and plains correctly.
4.6D	I can design an experiment to test the effect of force on an object.	3E	I can share in a cooperative group what I know about designing experiments.
5.7A	I will explore the processes that led to the formation of fossil fuels.	4F	I will use visual and contextual supports to read information about fossil fuel formation.
5.8A	The learner will differentiate between weather and climate.	5G	The learner will describe in writing the current weather and the climate of a given geographic area.
Middle School			
6.5C	We can differentiate between elements and compounds.	1G	We will use formal/informal English to describe the difference between elements and compounds.
6.12D	The student will classify organisms into kingdoms based on their characteristics.	2I	The student will demonstrate listening comprehension by classifying organisms into kingdoms based on a description read aloud by the teacher.
7.4A	I will use appropriate tools to collect information during experiments.	3G	I will express opinions about which tool to use by using the sentence stem, "I think the best choice is _____ because…"
7.6B	The learner will distinguish between physical and chemical changes in matter in the digestive system.	1C	The learner will create a graphic organizer to show the distinctions between physical and chemical changes in matter in the digestive system.
8.9B	The student will identify the plate tectonic interactions required to form a crustal feature.	5F	The student will use the R.A.F.T. strategy to relate plate tectonics to the formation of a crustal feature by taking on the role of one plate writing a letter (format) to an adjacent plate (audience) about how they can work together to form a specific crustal feature (topic).
8.11D	I can explain how human activities affect the ocean systems.	4G	I can read and summarize newspaper articles about human affects on ocean systems.
High School			
IPC.4A	We will describe an object's motion.	5B	We will describe in writing an object's motion in terms of position, speed, displacement, and acceleration.
Bio.9A	The learner will distinguish between different types of biomolecules.	1C	The learner will use Personal Dictionary note cards to distinguish biomolecules with regards to structure and function.
Bio.9C	The student will identify the role of enzymes in the process of digestion.	3B	The student will utilize diagrams of how enzymes act on macromolecules to explain the process to a peer.
Chem.4D	I can classify matter as pure substances or mixtures through experimentation.	2D	I can listen to instructions and conduct an experiment to classify matter as pure substances or mixtures.
Phys.6E	The learner will describe how the macroscopic properties of a thermodynamic system are related to the molecular level of matter.	1G	The learner will distinguish between formal and informal English to describe how the macroscopic properties of a thermodynamic system are related to the molecular level of matter.
Enviro.9H	We will analyze different views on the existence of global warming.	4G	We will utilize shared reading to analyze different views on the existence of global warming.

ELPS Lesson Plan Template

Grade: Topic:

Subject: Date:

Content Objective *(Aligned with TEKS)*:	Language Objective *(Aligned with ELPS)*:
Vocabulary:	Visuals, Materials & Texts:

Activities	**Review & Checks for Understanding:** *(Response Signals, Writing, Self-Assessment Student Products, etc,)*
Activating Prior Knowledge *(Processes, Stems, and Strategies)*: **Building Vocabulary and Concept Knowledge** *(Processes, Stems, and Strategies)*: **Structured Conversation and Writing** *(Processes, Stems, and Strategies):*	

ELPS Lesson Plan Sample (Elementary)

Grade: _____ 4th _____   **Topic:** _____ Conductors vs. Insulators _____

Subject: _____ Science _____   **Date:** _____

Content Objective *(Aligned with TEKS)*: (6B and C)	Language Objective *(Aligned with ELPS)*: (1E)
I can use an electrical circuit to test if a material is a conductor or an insulator.	I can demonstrate my understanding of conductors vs. insulators both verbally and in writing.
Vocabulary: Electricity, conductor, insulator	**Visuals, Materials & Texts:** Wire, battery, light bulb, a variety of materials to test including both conductors and insulators such as paperclips, rubber bands, coins, plastic toys, erasers, aluminum foil, etc.

Activities	Review & Check for Understanding: *(Response Signals, Writing, Student Product, Student Self-assessment.)*
Activating Prior Knowledge *(Processes, Stems, Strategies)*: Teacher Questions<ul><li>What does insulator mean to you?</li><li>What do we need to make a light bulb light up?</li><li>How can we use a simple circuit to test if a material conducts electricity?</li></ul>Whip Around Expressing prior knowledge stems : *Insulator means…* *I can make a light bulb light up with….* *I can use a _____ to test materials by_____.* **Building Vocabulary and Concept Knowledge *(Processes, Stems, Strategies)*:**<ul><li>Use PowerPoint to introduce the lesson's key vocabulary</li><li>Students create a two-tab folded paper organizer with tabs labeled Insulators or Conductors to record observations and take notes.</li><li>Students use a simple electrical circuit to test various materials to determine if they are conductors or insulators.</li><li>Students predict if an object will conduct electricity or not before testing the object.</li></ul>Descriptive language stems: *The word _____ means…* *An example of the word _____ is…* *The picture I drew for the word _____ is…* *I think most _____ are made of _____* *The best conductor I tested was _____ because _____* *I predict a _____ will (or will not) conduct electricity because _____.* **Structured Conversation and Writing *(Processes, Stems, Strategies)*:** Write, Inside/Outside Circles Persuasive Language Stems: *My prediction is correct because…* *I do/do not think her guess is correct because…* *I do/do not think ____ conducts ____ because…*	Orally review previous lesson (on electrical circuits) Do students know what insulation and insulators are, or is there a need to build background knowledge? Agree/Disagree Listen to student conversations Provide sufficient wait time for students to formulate responses Observe student work Are students' predictions reasonable? Are students using the lesson's vocabulary to express their thoughts? Review key content by showing students objects and having them predict their ability to conduct electricity by writing the answer on response boards

ELPS Lesson Plan Sample (Middle School)

Grade: 6th **Topic:** Calculating Density

Subject: Science **Date:**

Content Objective *(Aligned with TEKS):* **(6.6B)** I can calculate density to identify an unknown substance.	**Language Objective** *(Aligned with ELPS):* **(3D)** I can describe how to calculate the density of liquids, regular solids, or irregular solids in order to identify an unknown substance.
Vocabulary: Density, mass, volume, fluid displacement	**Visuals, Materials & Texts:** Lab materials, calculators, chart paper

Activities

Activating Prior Knowledge *(Processes, Stems, Strategies)*:
Teacher Questions
- What do you know about density?
- What is something that is very dense?
- What is something that is not very dense?
- What happens to a very dense thing in water?

Graffiti Write
Expressing prior knowledge stems :
Density is...
One thing I remember about density is...
An example of a something that is very dense is...
Density is not the same as...
A very dense thing in water will...

Building Vocabulary and Concept Knowledge *(Processes, Stems, Strategies)*:
- Introduce the lesson's vocabulary by following the first three steps of the Six Step Vocabulary Process.
- Provide each group of students with a sample liquid, a regular solid, and an irregular solid (must fit in a graduated cylinder). Tell students they are going to quantify the density of these forms using the formula: density is equal to mass divided by volume.
- Ask students to discuss with their group how they can measure the mass and volume of each substance given.
- Have groups share their methods with the class. Share methods they do not mention, as it is unlikely they will know about fluid displacement.
- Allow students to practice each method with new materials.
- Use Inside/Outside circle to facilitate a review of the concepts and vocabulary.
- Provide each group with five different liquids that they must pour into a column in the correct order with most dense on the bottom. Suggestions: molasses, salt water, water, alcohol and oil (use food coloring as needed to define layers).

Descriptive language stems:
_____ means...
To measure mass I need to...
To find the volume of a regular solid I can...
To find the volume of a liquid I can...
To find the volume of an irregular solid I need to...

Structured Conversation and Writing *(Processes, Stems, Strategies)*:
Write, Think , Pair , Share
Persuasive Language Stems:
I think we need to pour the _____ in first (next, last) because...

Review & Check for Understanding:
(Response Signals, Writing, Student Product, Student Self-assessment.)

Solicit prior knowledge through questioning.

Listen to student conversations

Observe student work

Do students recognize different methods for obtaining volume in order to calculate density?

Given new materials, do students describe the proper method for obtaining volume?

Can students properly predict the order of liquids in a density column?

Outcome Sentences
I learned...
I liked...
I wonder...
I think...

ELPS Lesson Plan Sample (High School)

Grade: _____ Biology _____   **Topic:** _____ Cell Differentiation _____

Subject: _____ Science _____   **Date:** _____

Content Objective *(Aligned with TEKS)*: (Biology.11A) SWBAT describe one internal feedback mechanism in humans.	Language Objective *(Aligned with ELPS)*: (3E) SWBAT orally describe one internal feedback mechanism in humans by participating in a <u>Read, Write, Pair, Share</u> activity.
Vocabulary: Internal feedback mechanism, feedback, homeostasis	**Visuals, Materials & Texts:** <u>Hi/Lo</u> or adapted <u>readings</u> about different human, internal feedback mechanisms.

Activities	Review & Check for Understanding: *(Response Signals, Writing, Student Product, Student Self-assessment.)*

Activating Prior Knowledge *(Processes, Stems, Strategies)*:
    Under what circumstances must our bodies work to maintain a stable environment?
    What might cause our bodies to be out of balance?
 	
Expressing prior knowledge stems:
    When I _____, my body must work to maintain a stable environment by _____.
    When I get _____ my body tells me to _____.
 	
Building Vocabulary and Concept Knowledge *(Processes, Stems, Strategies)*:
• Provide student pairs with readings and ask them to <u>Partner Read</u> the material.
• Each pair of students uses their reading to create a mini-poster about their internal feedback mechanism. Each student will need his or her own copy of the material to use later.
• Students should practice <u>Retelling</u> the information to their partner using their poster and the following stem:
    My poster is about...
 	
Descriptive language stems:
    When _____ happens the body responds by _____.
    Our reading was about...
    My poster shows how...
 	
Structured Conversation and Writing *(Processes, Stems, Strategies)*:
<u>Think, Pair, Share</u> – Students should find a new partner that had a different feedback mechanism and share information. Once they have shared they will trade papers and go on to describe another student's work to a new partner.
Persuasive Language Stems:
    My poster is about...
    This poster shows...
    I think this feedback mechanism is important because...
	Orally review previous material related to human anatomy by having students participate in a Carousel sharing activity
	
	Listen to student conversations
	
	Observe student work
	
	Check posters for labels and accuracy
	
	Do students accurately describe the internal feedback mechanism that was just described to them?

ELPS Lesson Plan Activity Guide
(subsection c)

Instructional Strategies	ELPS Student Expectation Summaries	Classroom Strategies/Techniques	
Activating Prior Knowledge	1A Use prior knowledge to learn new language 1F Use accessible language to learn new language 4D Use pre-reading supports 4E Read linguistically content area accommodated materials 4F Use visual, contextual, and peer supports to read text	• Anticipation Guides • Advance Organizers • Backwards Book walk • Chunking Input • Graffiti Write • Graphic Organizers	• KWL • Math Sort • Prediction Café • Scanning • Vis. Literacy Frames • Visuals/Video
Building Vocabulary and Concept Knowledge	1E Use and reuse basic and academic language 1C Use techniques to learn new vocabulary 1H Expand repertoire of learning strategies to acquire language 2B Recognize English sound system in new vocabulary 2F Derive meaning from a variety of media 3A Practice speaking using English sound system in new vocabulary 3B Use new vocabulary in oral communication 4A Learn relationships of sounds and letters in English 4B Recognize directionality of English text 4G Show comprehension of English text individually and in groups 4H Read silently with comprehension 4I Show comprehension through basic reading skills 4J Show comprehension through inferential skills 4K Show comprehension through analytical skills 4C Develop sight vocabulary and language structures	• Cloze Sentences • Concept Attainment • Comprehension Strategies • Creating Words • Dirty Laundry • DRTA • Expert/Novice • Guess Your Corner • Hi-lo readers • Homophone/ • Homograph Sort • List/Sort/Label • Mix and Match	• Nonlinguistic Rep. • Prefixes, Suffixes, and Roots • QtA • QAR • SQP2RS • Self-Assessment of Word Knowledge • Word Analysis • Think Alouds • Word Generation • Word Sorts • Word Walls • Vocabulary Alive
Structured Conversation	1B Monitor language with self-corrective techniques 1G Distinguish between formal and informal English 2D Monitor understanding and seek clarification 2E Use support to confirm and enhance understanding 1D Speak using learning strategies 2C Learn language heard in interactions and instruction 2I Demonstrate listening comprehension 2A Distinguish sound and intonation 2G Understand general meaning, main points, and details 2H Understand implicit ideas and information 3C Speak using a variety of sentence structures 3D Speak using grade level content area vocabulary in context 3E Share in cooperative groups 3F Ask and give information using common and content area vocabulary 3G Express opinions, ideas, and feelings orally 3H Narrate, describe ,and explain orally 3I Use oral language for formal and informal purposes 3J Respond orally to a variety of media sources	• Accountable Conversation Stems • Instr. Conversation • Literature Circles • Num. Heads Together • Perspective-Based Writing • Question Answer Relationship (QAR)	• QSSSA • Response Triads • Reciprocal Teaching • Structured Conv. • Structured Academic Controversy • Think, Pair, Share, • Tiered Resp. Stems • W.I.T.
Writing	5A Learn relationships between sounds and letters when writing 5B Write using basic and content area vocabulary 5C Spell familiar English words accurately 5D Edit writing for standard grammar and usage 5E Employ complex grammatical structures in content area 5F Write using variety of sentence structures and words 5G Narrate, describe, and explain in writing	• Book Reviews • Contextualized Grammar Instruction • Chat Room • Daily Oral Language • Double Entry Journals • Genre Analysis and Imitation	• Learning Logs • RAFT • Roundtable • Sentence Stems • Sentence Mark Up • Sentence Sorts • Summarization Frames • Unit Study for ELLs

Conducting an Inquiry Based Experiment

Content Objective(s) (Aligned with TEKS)	Language Objective(s) (Aligned with ELPS)
We will conduct scientific experiments and draw conclusions from data.	We will conduct scientific experiments and use our data to express our conclusion by stating If _____ then _____ because _____ .

Vocabulary		Visuals, Materials & Texts
Science Specific	**General**	• Concepts suited for inquiry activities
Will vary depending on content TEKS addressed by teacher.	Independent Variable Dependent Variable Control Hypothesis	• Conducting an Inquiry Based Experiment – Student Notebook Layout (all responses will be recorded in their science notebooks)

Instructions

Notes
- Students should have a basic understanding of the content being covered prior to the inquiry investigation.
- The content or concept being covered should be on grade level and appropriate for classroom experimentation. For example, factors affecting plant growth can be studied in the classroom, while elements found within the atmospheres of other planets is a topic that students can only answer through research.
- The general process for conducting an inquiry-based experiment may look different depending on grade level. In primary grades this may be a whole-class, teacher-led process with a class notebook being utilized.

Advanced Preparation:
- Brainstorm possible student questions and experiments in order to gather appropriate materials. A suggested materials list may be given to the students so they know what they may and may not use.
- Determine ahead of time if there are any possible experiments that are unsafe and would not be allowed. Students should be informed of these limitations before beginning the planning process. For example, students may be allowed to use plants or even insects to conduct an experiment but vertebrates are not allowed.

Process
1. Begin by asking students to create a T chart with one side title "I Know" and the other "I Wonder."
2. Students then brainstorm with a group (although individual students may personalize the list that is in their notebook) a list of things that they know and wonder about the concept being covered.
3. Randomly call on students to share their list with others in class, writing responses on a piece of chart paper or a section of the board.
4. Students then work with their group and choose their top three "I Wonders" and write them as questions.
5. Discuss with students how a controlled experiment works. Remind them we must only have one independent variable that we, as scientists, are going to manipulate or change in some way. Students must also be aware of the need for control groups (groups which are not subject to the independent variable).
6. Given those guidelines, each group chooses one question to answer experimentally.
7. Students predict what they think will happen. Students are not writing a hypothesis at this time, as background information and experimentation are required to write a hypothesis. Instead students should complete the stem "I predict _____ because_____ ."
8. Students then brainstorm a list of all possible considerations for their experiment including materials, controls, and most importantly, what data and observations (the dependent variables) will be collected and how. Students should also create a data table to record their data and observations.
9. Students should then write their procedure and submit it for teacher approval. Procedures may need to change as the experiment continues. Alternatively, students who are less proficient in English may choose to draw their experiment but all steps and materials must be clearly labeled.
10. Students are then given time to conduct the experiment and record data and observations. Students should graph their data, appropriate to the grade level and experiment.
11. When the experiments are complete, students should analyze their data for trends. Once trends have been identified students should write their conclusions, including their hypothesis. The hypothesis should be written as an If___ then___ because___ statement. For example: If sprouted corn seeds are watered with vinegar, then they will grow slower than corn grown in water, because the acid in the vinegar will stunt the plants growth.
12. Next students reflect on the inquiry procedure in their science notebooks.
13. Review key vocabulary and content and language objectives.

Science Activities that Promote Language Development

Conducting an Inquiry Based Experiment – Science Notebook Layout

Topic: Date:

I Know	I Wonder

Questions: (students will need to star, highlight, etc. the question they choose for the experiment)

Prediction: I predict _____ will _____ because _____.

Things we must take into account (our considerations):

Independent Variable:

Controls:

Dependent Variable:

Procedure:

Data and Observations:

Trends:

Conclusions:

Hypothesis: If _____ then _____ because _____.

Reflections:

Science Activities that Promote Language Development

Concepts Suited for Inquiry Based Experiments
Note: This is not an exhaustive list

Grade Level/Course	TEKS and Concept
K	K.9B Living organisms have basic needs such as water, nutrients, sunlight, and space for plants
1	1.5B Predict and identify changes in materials caused by heating and cooling
2	2.6A Investigate the effects of an object by increasing or decreasing amounts of light, heat, and sound energy such as how heat melts butter
3	3.5C Predict, observe, and record changes in the state of matter caused by heating or cooling
4	4.6D Design an experiment to test the effect of force on an object
5	5.5D Identify changes that can occur in the physical properties of the ingredients of solutions
6	6.9B Verify through investigations that thermal energy moves in a predictable pattern
7	7.13A Investigate how organisms respond to external stimuli such as phototropism
8	8.5E Investigate how evidence of chemical reactions indicate the way new substances with different properties are formed
Integrated Physics and Chemistry	IPC.5D Investigate the law of conservation of energy
Biology	Biology 11.B Investigate and analyze how organisms, populations, and communities respond to external factors
Chemistry	Chemistry.10F Investigate factors that influence solubilities and rates of dissolution
Physics	Physics.5G Investigate and describe the relationship between electric and magnetic fields
Aquatic Science	Aquatic Science.5A-D Long-term studies on local aquatic environments (independent variable could possibly be testing upstream and downstream from a water treatment plant)
Astronomy	Astronomy.8C Recognize that the angle of incidence of sunlight determines the concentration of solar energy received on Earth
Earth and Space Science	ESS.14B Investigate how the atmosphere is heated from Earth's surface due to absorption of solar energy
Environmental Systems	Environmental Systems.4E Measure the concentration of solute, solvent, and solubility of dissolved substances and describe their impact on an ecosystem

Science Activities that Promote Language Development

Science Happens

Content Objective(s) (Aligned with TEKS)	Language Objective(s) (Aligned with ELPS)
SWBAT analyze and critique scientific explanations found in real world print and relate the impact of research on scientific thought and society.	SWBAT read and summarize in 2-3 sentences, information obtained from science related real world print, such as newspaper or internet articles.

Vocabulary		Visuals, Materials & Texts	
Science Specific	General	• Newspaper	
Variable	Summarize	• Internet access	
Control		• World Map	
Hypothesis		• String	
		• Tape	

Instructions

Preparation
- Place the world map in a spacious area in the classroom or hallway where articles can be posted around it.
- Place the string and tape near the map for easy access.
- Determine possible sources for articles including newspapers and appropriate internet sites. Consider including internet sites/reading material that supports the various reading levels of your students, such as "science news for kids."

Process
1. Give a student or pair of students time to find and read an article related to science.
2. As students read the article, instruct them to highlight important ideas and how the particular science impacts society.
3. Students should be given the opportunity to ask questions about the article, either verbally or in writing, and receive responses from the teacher during the next class period.
4. Students should write a summary of the article in 2-3 sentences and submit the summary for review.
5. Once approved, the article and summary should be posted near the map with a string connecting the article to the geographic location of the science being conducted (either field site or location of laboratory conducting research).
6. As time allows, students may present their summary to the class or be given time to read the summaries posted by other students.

Based on an activity designed by Stef Paramoure. Used with permission.

Science Activities that Promote Language Development

Which Way Did It Go? A Walk Through the Nitrogen Cycle

Content Objective(s) (Aligned with TEKS)	Language Objective(s) (Aligned with ELPS)
I will explore and describe the flow of matter through the nitrogen cycle.	I will draw a diagram showing the flow of matter through the nitrogen cycle and explain the process in a short essay.

Vocabulary		Visuals, Materials & Texts	
Science Specific	General	• Nitrogen cycle cubes • Station labels • Handout: A walk through the nitrogen cycle	• Colored pencils and/or markers • Blank copy paper
Nitrogen Cycle Nitrogen Fixation Denitrification	Cycle Process Remain		

Instructions

Notes
- While this activity focuses on the nitrogen cycle, similar activities exist and can be found on the Internet for the water cycle, the carbon cycle, etc.
- In this activity, students travel through various stations around the classroom to learn about the nitrogen cycle. As an alternate to this activity, students may work in an assigned group without traveling. However, this version requires each group to have all five cubes: atmosphere, soil, plants, animals, and water cycle.

Preparation
- Prepare at least one set of the nitrogen cycle cubes by printing the cubes' outline on cardstock, cutting them out, and folding and taping them to form the cubes. If you want to increase the number of students traveling through the various stations and reduce wait time between rolls, consider placing more than one cube at each station.
- Create labels for each of the different stations you are setting up. The stations are atmosphere, soil, plants, animals, and water cycle.
- Copy the handout, "A Walk through the Nitrogen Cycle," for each student.

Process
1. Begin by asking students what a cycle is? Solicit responses from several students using the following stem:
   A cycle is _____.
2. Once the concept of a cycle has been established, let students know that they are going to explore the nitrogen cycle by rolling a series of cubes, record the information obtained from the cube onto their handout, and following the instructions to "remain" or "head to" another station as indicated on the side of the cube that is facing up.
3. Explain the processes of nitrogen fixation and denitrification without showing a diagram of the nitrogen cycle. Preview and review any other vocabulary from the cubes that students may not be familiar with, including remain, head to, excreted, incorporated, etc.
4. Show students the cubes, and have several students read the instructions from the handout aloud. Walk students through an example of the activity by rolling a cube, marking on a sample handout what should be recorded, remaining or moving to a different station, and then rolling the next cube.
5. Assign students a station where they will begin the rotations or have them select one. Ensure that the number of students starting at each station is roughly equal.
6. Allow students to work through the stations until most of them have traveled through six rolls.
7. Show students a diagram of the water cycle and review the important components, make sure to explain the labels and what is happening along each arrow.
8. Working in groups of 2-4 members, have students use the information from their handouts to construct a diagram of the nitrogen cycle. They must label and explain all the components of their diagram, including the arrows.
9. Have students take turns sharing their diagrams with each other in small groups or through a gallery walk.
10. Each student should write a short essay (length differentiated by ability level) summarizing the nitrogen cycle.

Science Activities that Promote Language Development

A Walk through the Nitrogen Cycle

Instructions: 1) Write the name of the station in the space indicated. 2) Roll the cube and record the information on the column labeled, "What happens to the nitrogen?" 3) Write whether you are remaining in your current station or heading to a different one on the column labeled "action." 4) Repeat steps one to four until your teacher asks you to stop.

Turn Number	Station Name	What Happens to the Nitrogen?	Action
Example: A	Atmosphere	You are caught up in a raindrop and fall to the ground.	Head to the water cycle
1			
2			
3			
4			
5			
6			
7			

Science Activities that Promote Language Development

A Walk Through the Nitrogen Cycle: Atmosphere Cube

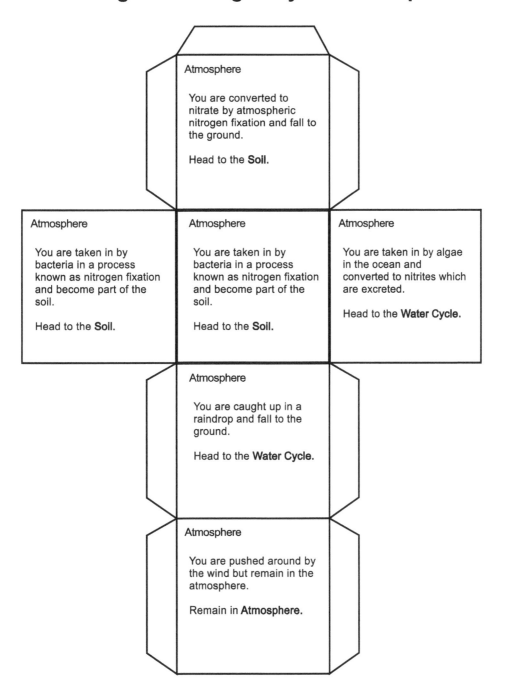

Atmosphere

You are converted to nitrate by atmospheric nitrogen fixation and fall to the ground.

Head to the **Soil.**

Atmosphere

You are taken in by bacteria in a process known as nitrogen fixation and become part of the soil.

Head to the **Soil.**

Atmosphere

You are taken in by bacteria in a process known as nitrogen fixation and become part of the soil.

Head to the **Soil.**

Atmosphere

You are taken in by algae in the ocean and converted to nitrites which are excreted.

Head to the **Water Cycle.**

Atmosphere

You are caught up in a raindrop and fall to the ground.

Head to the **Water Cycle.**

Atmosphere

You are pushed around by the wind but remain in the atmosphere.

Remain in **Atmosphere.**

Science Activities that Promote Language Development

A Walk Through the Nitrogen Cycle: Soil Cube

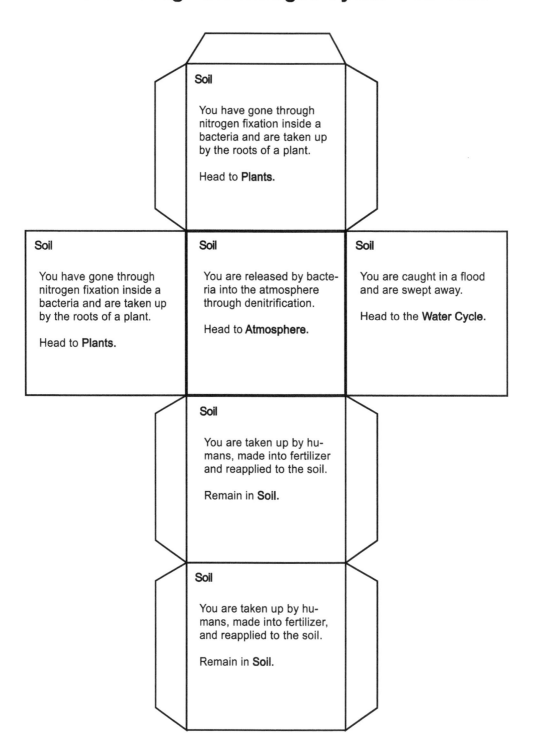

Soil

You have gone through nitrogen fixation inside a bacteria and are taken up by the roots of a plant.

Head to **Plants.**

Soil

You have gone through nitrogen fixation inside a bacteria and are taken up by the roots of a plant.

Head to **Plants.**

Soil

You are released by bacteria into the atmosphere through denitrification.

Head to **Atmosphere.**

Soil

You are caught in a flood and are swept away.

Head to the **Water Cycle.**

Soil

You are taken up by humans, made into fertilizer and reapplied to the soil.

Remain in **Soil.**

Soil

You are taken up by humans, made into fertilizer, and reapplied to the soil.

Remain in **Soil.**

A Walk Through the Nitrogen Cycle: Plants Cube

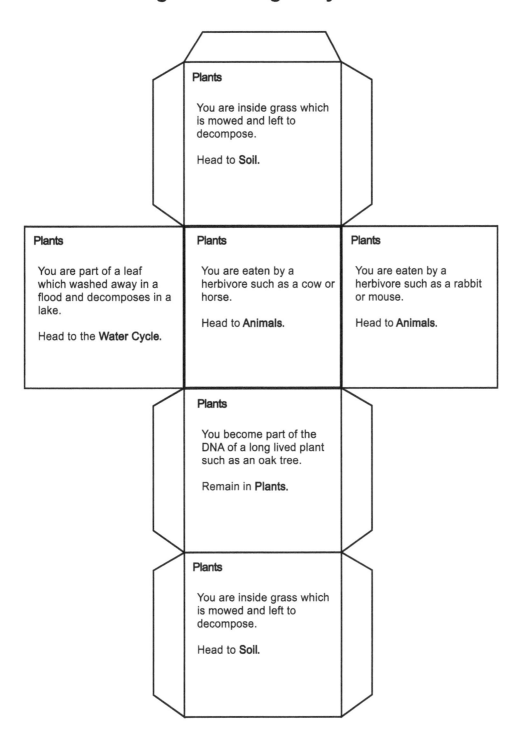

Plants

You are inside grass which is mowed and left to decompose.

Head to **Soil.**

Plants

You are part of a leaf which washed away in a flood and decomposes in a lake.

Head to the **Water Cycle.**

Plants

You are eaten by a herbivore such as a cow or horse.

Head to **Animals.**

Plants

You are eaten by a herbivore such as a rabbit or mouse.

Head to **Animals.**

Plants

You become part of the DNA of a long lived plant such as an oak tree.

Remain in **Plants.**

Plants

You are inside grass which is mowed and left to decompose.

Head to **Soil.**

A Walk Through the Nitrogen Cycle: Animals Cube

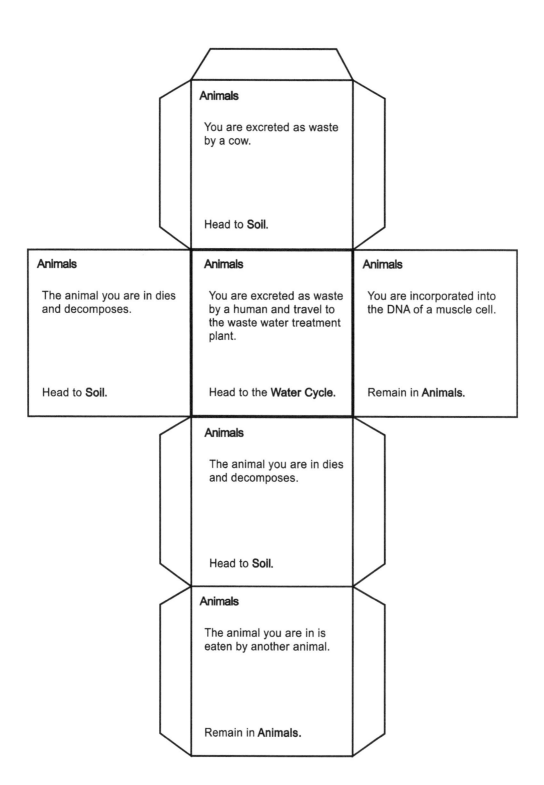

Animals

You are excreted as waste by a cow.

Head to **Soil.**

Animals

The animal you are in dies and decomposes.

Head to **Soil.**

Animals

You are excreted as waste by a human and travel to the waste water treatment plant.

Head to the **Water Cycle.**

Animals

You are incorporated into the DNA of a muscle cell.

Remain in **Animals.**

Animals

The animal you are in dies and decomposes.

Head to **Soil.**

Animals

The animal you are in is eaten by another animal.

Remain in **Animals.**

Science Activities that Promote Language Development

A Walk Through the Nitrogen Cycle: Water Cycle Cube

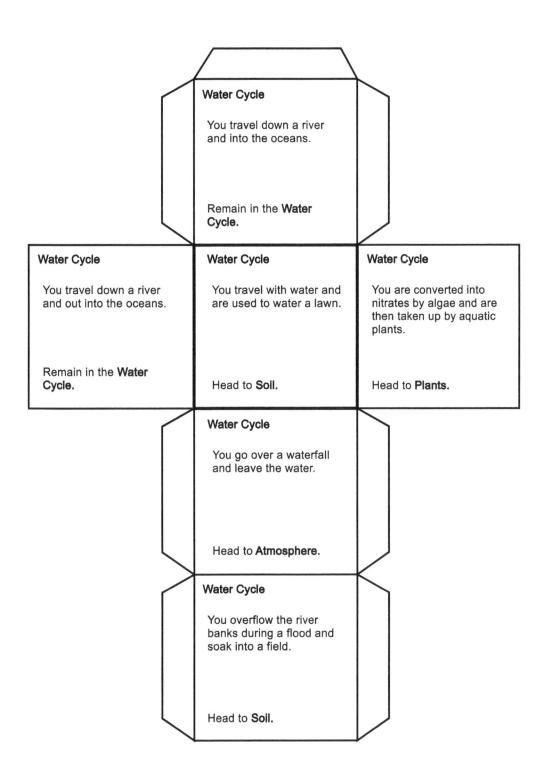

Water Cycle

You travel down a river and into the oceans.

Remain in the **Water Cycle.**

Water Cycle

You travel down a river and out into the oceans.

Remain in the **Water Cycle.**

Water Cycle

You travel with water and are used to water a lawn.

Head to **Soil.**

Water Cycle

You are converted into nitrates by algae and are then taken up by aquatic plants.

Head to **Plants.**

Water Cycle

You go over a waterfall and leave the water.

Head to **Atmosphere.**

Water Cycle

You overflow the river banks during a flood and soak into a field.

Head to **Soil.**

Science Activities that Promote Language Development

Putting the Pieces Together: Connection Card Sort

Content Objective(s) (Aligned with TEKS)	Language Objective(s) (Aligned with ELPS)
The learner will make connections between concepts such as how systems of the human body work together. (Objective will vary by grade level.)	The learner will orally describe the connections between concepts.

Vocabulary		Visuals, Materials & Texts	
Science Specific	General	• Connection Card Sort cards	
Depends on the grade level and set of cards used.	Connects Causes Results in Is not related to		

Instructions

Notes
- This activity is designed as a formative assessment after students have learned about the process or concepts involved in the card sort.
- Depending on the grade level, this may be a teacher-directed activity with students taking turns pulling cards out of a set and describing the connection between two cards. Otherwise, model the process once or twice before students do the activity with their partner/group.

Preparation
- Make sets of the connection card sorts as needed. In most cases, students should be able to work in groups of 2-3.

Process
1. Distribute the connection card sorts to each pair or group of students.
2. Have students glance through the sets and ask them what process or concepts they note on the card.
3. Students should make two stacks of cards with all the A cards in one stack and all the B cards in the other.
4. Students will take turns, first drawing a card from the A stack and then one from the B stack.
5. Students should then state how the two cards are connected or why they are not connected.
   _____ *connects/does not connect to* _____ *because…*
   Example: A student draws Cooling from the A stack and Condensation from the B stack. The student might say *Cooling connects to condensation because a gas condenses into a liquid when it cools.*
6. Cards are returned to the bottom of the stack, and the next student draws two cards and states the connection.
7. Students can also be required to write down their statements after discussing them with their partners.
8. Alternative Use: Students can also be asked to match cards from stack A with cards from stack B and write connecting statements for each set (or a certain number of sets) rather than pulling random cards.

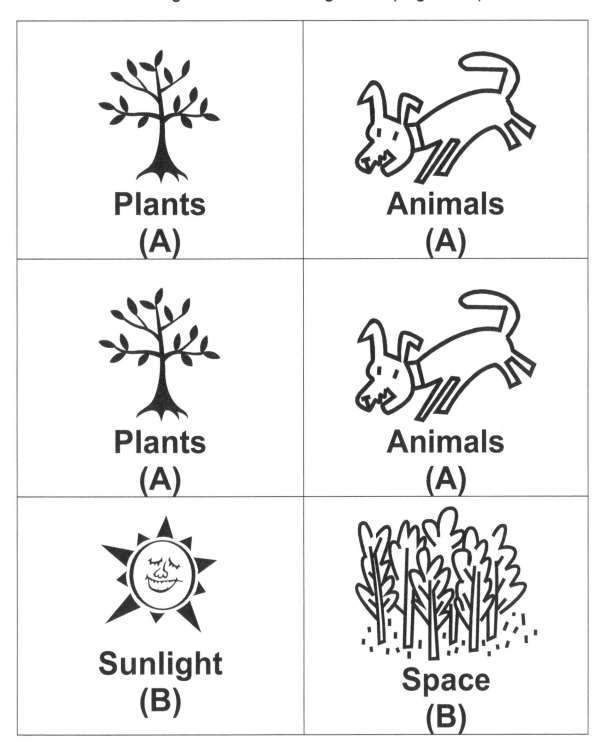

Food
(B)

Water
(B)

Shelter
(B)

Air
(B)

Nutrients
(B)

Science Activities that Promote Language Development

Putting the Pieces Together: Connection Card Sort
Grade 4 – Phase Changes (Page 1 of 2)

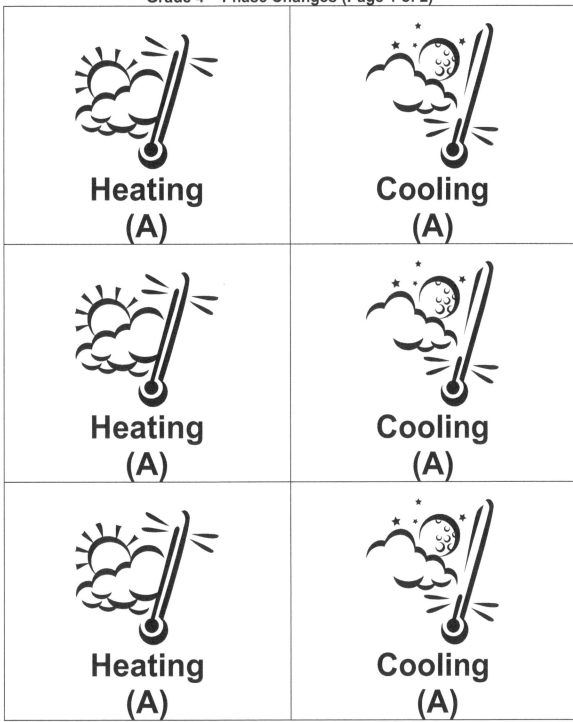

Heating (A)	**Cooling** (A)
Heating (A)	**Cooling** (A)
Heating (A)	**Cooling** (A)

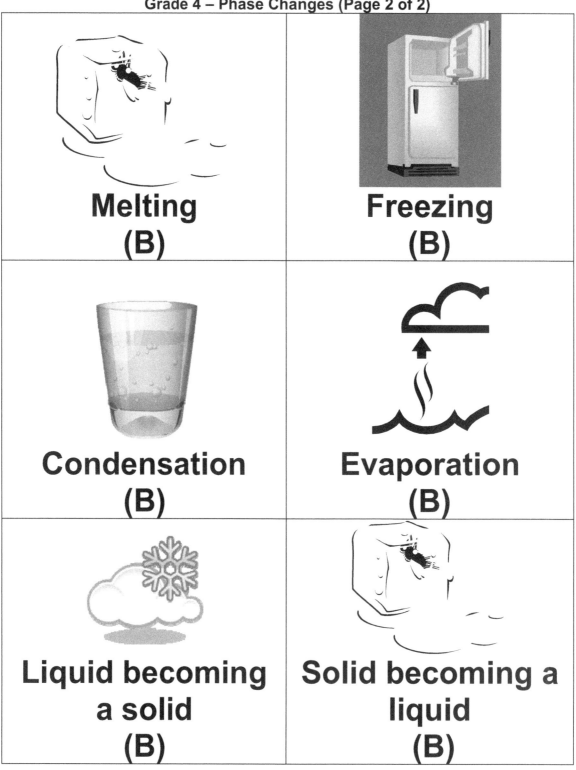

Melting (B)	**Freezing (B)**
Condensation (B)	**Evaporation (B)**
Liquid becoming a solid (B)	**Solid becoming a liquid (B)**

Putting the Pieces Together: Connection Card Sort
Biology – Human Systems (Page 1 of 2)

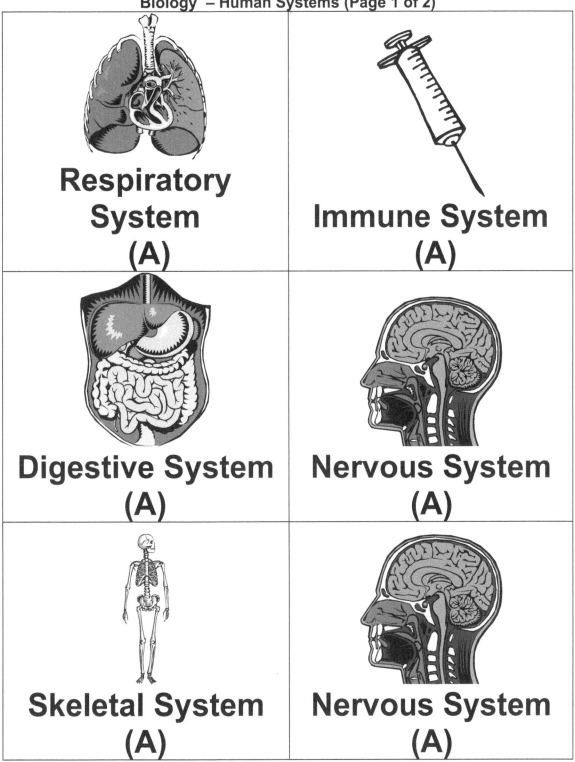

Respiratory System (A)	**Immune System (A)**
Digestive System (A)	**Nervous System (A)**
Skeletal System (A)	**Nervous System (A)**

Putting the Pieces Together: Connection Card Sort
Biology – Human Systems (Page 2 of 2)

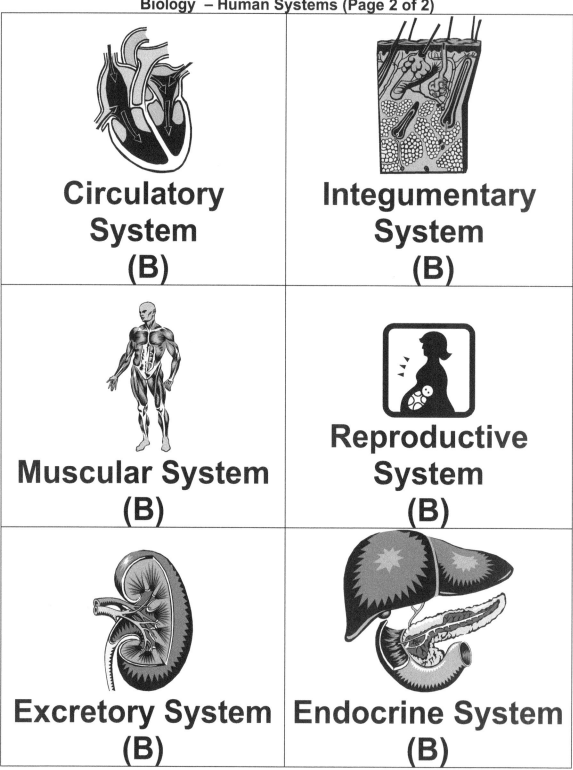

Circulatory System (B)

Integumentary System (B)

Muscular System (B)

Reproductive System (B)

Excretory System (B)

Endocrine System (B)

Sentence Stems and Activities Aligned to
Cross-Curricular Student Expectations
(subsection c)

Learning Strategies		
1(A) use prior knowledge and experiences to understand meanings in English	**Prior Knowledge** Teacher Questions • What do you know about...? • What do you remember about...? • What is an example of a...? • What is a non-example of a...? • What is a ...? • What is a type of ...? • What experience have you had with...? • What have you learned about...? • Close your eyes and think of ___. What do you see? • What does the picture/word/phrase remind you of? • What does ___ mean to you? • How can ___ be represented? • How have you used...? • What do you think the word ___ means? • Where in your daily life do you see (use, interact with, etc.)...? • Think about a time when you... Student Sentence Stems • I know.... • I remember... • An example of a ___ is... • A non-example of a _____ is... • A ___ is... • A type of ___ is... • An experience I have had with ___ is... • I learned... • I see... • The picture reminds me of... • ___ means... • A ___ can be represented with a... • I have used ___ to... • I think ___ means... • I see (use) _____ when I... • A time I used ___ was when...	• Anticipation Chat • Anticipation Guides • Insert Method • KWL • List/Group/Label • Pretest with a partner • Free Write • Card Sorts • Graffiti Write • Carousel Activity • Sculptorades
	Examples	
	PK-5 • I know a bus is **bigger** than a car. • A non-example of a **model** is looking at the moon through a telescope. • I learned **adaptations** help organisms survive. 6-8 • An example of a **law** is **Newton's first law of motion**. • I think **force** means to push or pull. • **Erosion** can be represented with a **model**. 9-12 • The pictures remind me of **light bulbs and switches.**. • I remember **elements** are found on the periodic table. • I use **chemicals** when I help clean the house.	

Sentence Stems and Activities Aligned to
Cross-Curricular Student Expectations
(subsection c)

Learning Strategies		
1(B) monitor oral and written language production and employ self-corrective techniques or other resources	**Self Corrective Techniques** Teacher Question/Statements <ul><li>Please say that again.</li><li>Please repeat.</li><li>What I hear you say is...</li><li>Does the statement sound correct to you?</li><li>Does it sound right/look right?</li><li>What did you notice?</li><li>What letter does the word ___ begin with?</li><li>What sound does ___ make?</li></ul> Student Sentence Stems <ul><li>I mean ...</li><li>I meant to say/write ...</li><li>I said...</li><li>Let me rephrase that.</li><li>Let me say that again.</li><li>The word I am thinking of looks like...</li><li>How do you pronounce this word?</li><li>How would I be able to check ...?</li></ul>	<ul><li>Accountable Conversation Questions</li><li>Oral Scaffolding</li><li>Think Alouds</li><li>Total Response Signals</li></ul>
	Examples PK-5 <ul><li>Student says, "I writed my **observations**." Teacher restates, "You wrote your **observations**." Student says, "Yes, <u>I wrote my observations.</u>"</li><li>Student says, "The Moon orbs the Earth ." Then self-corrects by saying, "I mean the **Moon orbits the Earth**."</li></ul>6-8 <ul><li>I meant to write, "**Safety rules are important**" instead of "<u>Rules safety is important</u>."</li></ul>9-12 <ul><li>How do you pronounce the word **polyatomic**?</li></ul>	
1(C) use strategic learning techniques such as concept mapping, drawing, memorizing, comparing, contrasting, and reviewing to acquire basic and grade-level vocabulary	**Drawing/Memorizing/Reviewing** Teacher Questions/Tasks <ul><li>What picture represents the word...?</li><li>What gesture could be used to represent...?</li><li>Create a rap song to remember...</li><li>Create a mnemonic device to memorize...</li><li>Match the words to their corresponding picture.</li><li>What strategy could you use to remember the meaning of...?</li></ul>	<ul><li>CALLA Approach</li><li>Concept Definition Map</li><li>Concept Mapping</li><li>Creating Analogies</li><li>Creating Words</li><li>Flash Card Review</li><li>Four Corners Vocabulary</li><li>Graffiti Write</li><li>Card Sorts</li></ul>

Sentence Stems and Activities Aligned to Cross-Curricular Student Expectations
(subsection c)

Learning Strategies		
1(C) continued	**Student Sentence Stems** • I drew a … • I can draw a ___ to represent a… • I can describe ___ by drawing a… • The model shows… • The picture represents the word… • The graph describes… • The symbol for ___ is… • The pattern is an example of a… • The word is ___ and it looks like this… • I memorized the ___ by remembering… • I decided to represent ___ this way because … • I know/don't know the words … • I'm familiar/not familiar with ___ • I will need to review … ### Concept Mapping **Teacher Questions** • What is the focus question of your concept map? • What important terms must you know to create a concept map of…? • What are the most important ideas in your concept map? • How does a concept map help you learn the meaning of…? • Why did you organize the information like that? **Student Sentence Stems** • The focus question is … • The terms I must know are… • The most important idea is… • ___ is related to ___. • Some examples of a ___ are … • A non-example is… ### Comparing/Contrasting **Teacher Questions** • What is the difference between…? • How are ___ and ___ the same? • Why do you think they are the same/different? **Student Sentence Stems** • A ___ has ___. • A ___ is ___. • A similarity is… • A difference is… • A ___ has ___, but a ___ has ___. • ___ and ___ both have ___. • An attribute ___ and ___ have in common is… • A property ___ and ___ don't share in common is… • ___ is the same as ___ because they are both … • ___ is different from ___ because … • ___ is similar to ___ because … • I think they are the same/different because…	• Multiple Representations • Graphic Organizer • Personal Dictionary • Scanning • Six Step Vocabulary Process • Total Physical Response (TPR) • Total Response Signals • Vocabulary Alive • Vocabulary Game Shows • Word Play • Word Sorts

Sentence Stems and Activities Aligned to Cross-Curricular Student Expectations
(subsection c)

Learning Strategies		
1(C) continued	Examples	
	PK-5 • I drew a picture to show the **cloud coverage**. • The model shows the **life cycle** of a frog. • The most important idea in the concept map is **basic needs**. • An ice cube is a **solid**. Soda is a **liquid**. **6-8** • I memorized **the order of the planets** by remembering <u>My Very Excellent Mother Just Sent Us Nachos.</u> • The word is **kinetic** and it looks like this (student waves arms and jumps up and down to show motion). • The **Sun** and the **Earth** both have layers inside them. **9-12** • I can describe **reflection** by drawing a ball bouncing off a wall. • **Photosynthesis** is related to **respiration**. • I used a three-circle Venn diagram to show how **conduction**, **convection**, and **radiation** are related.	
1(D) speak using learning strategies such as requesting assistance, employing non-verbal cues, and using synonyms and circumlocution (conveying ideas by defining or describing when exact English words are not known)	**Requesting Assistance** Teacher Questions • Did you understand the question? • Do you want me to repeat the question? • What gesture can you use to alert me to speak slower? Student Sentence Stems • Can you help me ...? • I don't understand ... • Would you please repeat/rephrase that...? • Would you please say that again a little slower? • Would you please explain ...? **Synonyms/Circumlocution** Teacher Questions • What other word can be used for the word ___? • What is an example of a ___? • What is a word that means the same as ___? • Describe the word you are thinking about. • What does the word/concept remind you of? Student Sentence Stems • It's the same as ... • ___ means the same as ___. • Another word for ___ is ___. • ___ is the same as the symbol ___. • A synonym for the word ___ is ___. • A ___ is a ___. • It's similar to ... • It includes ... • The word I am thinking of looks like...	• CALLA Approach • Accountable Conversation Questions • Expert/Novice • Instructional Scaffolding • Think, Pair, Share • Total Physical Response (TPR) • Vocabulary Alive

Sentence Stems and Activities Aligned to
Cross-Curricular Student Expectations
(subsection c)

Learning Strategies		
1(D) continued	Examples	
	PK-5 • Another word for **decay** is **decompose**. • The word I am thinking of means the same as lightning bolt. 6-8 • A synonym for the word **convert** is **change**. • **Water** means the same as **H_2O.** 9-12 • **Chemical change** means the same as **chemical reaction**. • The word I am thinking of reminds me of a rainbow.	
1(E) internalize new basic and academic language by using and reusing it in meaningful ways in speaking and writing activities that build concept and language attainment	**Concept Attainment with New Words** Teacher Questions/Tasks • How would you categorize the words/ pictures? • What are the attributes of...? • Classify the .... Student Sentence Stems • A characteristic is... • A characteristic of ___ and ___ is... • One characteristic/attribute of ___ is ... • The group has... • I would classify this word/concept under ___ category. • The patterns have in common... • All ___ are ... • All ___ have ... • All ___ are not ... • All ___ do not have ... • ___ is an example of ___ because... • ___ is a non-example of ___ because ... • Another example might be ___ because .... **Language Attainment with New Words** Teacher Questions/Tasks • Share with a partner what you know about the word... • Write words/examples associated with the word... • Is there another word for ___? • What science term have you learned that describes ___? • What does ___ represent? • Use the words ___, ___, and ___ in a complete sentence. Student Sentence Stems • ___ means ... • ___ represents ___. • A ___ is an attribute of a ___. • Another word for ___ is ___. • The ___ describes ... • A science term that describes ___ is ___. • I can use the word ___ when ... • I would not use the word ___ when ... • I might be able to use the word ___ when ___ because ... • I probably would not use the word ___ when ___ because ...	• CALLA Approach • Conga Line • Concept Attainment • Creating Words • Concept Definition Map • Creating Analogies • Dirty Laundry • Fold the Line • Group Response with a White Board • Instructional Conversation • Multiple Representations Graphic Organizer • Question, Signal, Stem, Share, Assess • Structured Academic Controversy • Think, Pair, Share • Whip Around • Word Sorts

Sentence Stems and Activities Aligned to Cross-Curricular Student Expectations
(subsection c)

Learning Strategies		
1(E) continued	**Examples**	
	PK-5 • Another word for **softness** is **pliability**. • All **traits** are not **inherited.** **6-8** • A science term that describes **non-living things** is **abiotic.** • I would use the word **organism** when talking about a tree, my dog, or myself. **9-12** • The **reactants** describe the **substances undergoing a change**. • Some characteristics of **a wave** include **frequency**, **wavelength**, and **amplitude**.	
1(F) use accessible language and learn new and essential language in the process	**Using Accessible Language** Teacher Questions • The word you are thinking of is... • What you are trying to say is... • What I hear you say is... • Will you repeat this word with me? Student Sentence Stems • I think... • The answer is... • The pattern is... • The process is... • I need to say ... • To find out how to say __ I can look at ... • Will you please explain what ___ means? • I can use resources such as ___ to remember how to say ...	• Accountable Conversation Questions • CALLA Approach • Chat Room • Creating Words • Dirty Laundry • Expert/Novice • Instructional Scaffolding • Think Alouds • Vocabulary Alive
	Examples	
	PK-5 • Student says, "I think the sandy **dirt** holds more water." Teacher says, "What I hear you say is that the sandy **soil** holds more water." **6-8** • The answer is **all organisms are composed of cells**. **9-12** • To find out how to say **the light bends**, I can look at my notes or ask a friend.	

Sentence Stems and Activities Aligned to
Cross-Curricular Student Expectations
(subsection c)

Learning Strategies		
1(G) demonstrate an increasing ability to distinguish between formal and informal English and an increasing knowledge of when to use each one commensurate with grade-level learning expectations	**Formal and Informal English** Teacher Questions • What word could you use instead of ___? • What word would you use to describe ___ to a friend? • What word would you use to describe ___ to a math teacher? Student Sentence Stems • The ___ has ...... • I would describe ___ to a friend by saying... • At school, we say ... • I would describe this to someone in my own words by saying/writing ... • I would describe that using mathematical language by saying ... **Examples** PK-5 • The cow eats the grass. **vs.** The cow consumes the grass. • I found the length. **vs.** I measured the length. 6-8 • The thing has many cells. **vs.** The organism is multicellular. • The land has been eaten away. **vs.** The land has eroded. • The atoms on both sides are equal. **vs.** The reaction is balanced. 9-12 • Energy was changed. **vs.** Energy was converted. • I would describe DNA to a friend by saying it is the molecule that carries the instructions for life.	• Brick and Mortar Cards • Card Sorts • Discussion Starter Cards • Formal/Informal Pairs • Mix and Match • Radio Talk Show • Same Scene Twice • Sentence Sort
1(H) develop and expand repertoire of learning strategies such as reasoning inductively or deductively, looking for patterns in language, and analyzing sayings and expressions commensurate with grade-level learning expectations	**Deductive Reasoning** Teacher Questions • What is given in the problem? • What questions can we ask to investigate this further? • The scientific law says... • If ___ is true, then we can state ...? Student Sentence Stems • All ___ have ___. ___ has ___. ___ must be a ___. • ___ has ___ and ___. ___ must be an example of ___. • All ___ have... • So it must be an example of ...	• Instructional Conversation • Perspective-Based Writing • Question, Signal, Stem, and Share • Structured Conversation

Sentence Stems and Activities Aligned to
Cross-Curricular Student Expectations
(subsection c)

Learning Strategies	
1(H) continued	**Inductive Reasoning**
	Teacher Questions
	• What can you conclude from the pattern?
	• What observations did you make?
	• Why did you group these ___ together?
	• What is a characteristic all ___ have/had in common?
	Student Sentence Stems
	• A counter example is...
	• A generalization is...
	• A conclusion is...
	• A conclusion I can make from the ___ is...
	• All ___ had the characteristic(s) of...
	• If the pattern continues, I think it will...
	• All the ___ we saw were/had ...
	• So all ___ probably are/have...
	• Every example we observed was/had ...
	• So we can infer that all ___ are/have...
	• If ___ works for ___, maybe ___ will work for...
	Patterns in Language
	Analyzing Sayings/Expressions
	Teacher Question
	• What are words/expressions I often use?
	• How can we write a chemical equation as a sentence?
	Student Sentence Stems
	• The answer is...
	• The expression that best describes ___ is...
	• The relationship between ___ and ___ is...
	• One pattern I noticed was ...
	• I think the word ___ means...
	• One word/expression that was used a lot was...

Examples
PK-5
• Living things need food and water. My dog needs food and water. My dog must be living.
6-8
• My inference is the water cycle never ends.
9-12
• One pattern I noticed was all the elements in a group have the same number of valence electrons.

Sentence Stems and Activities Aligned to Cross-Curricular Student Expectations
(subsection c)

Listening		
2(A) distinguish sounds and intonation patterns of English with increasing ease	**Sounds and Intonation Patterns** Teacher Questions • Did I ask a question or make a statement? Why? • Can you tell ___ and ___ apart? How? • Can you distinguish between ___ and ___? • Why did I stress the word___? • Is the word ___ spelled with a ___ or a ___? Student Sentence Stems • What you said sounded like a ___ because... • Are you telling me or asking me? • I can tell ___ apart from ___. • I can distinguish between ___ and ___. • I can't distinguish between ___ and ___. • ___ sounds different than ___. • The word ___ and ___ sound the same to me. • You said the word ___. It starts with... • I think that word starts with the letter (is spelled) ___ because ... • You stressed the word ___ because ... • You did not stress the word ___ because ... • To change the meaning of this sentence I could stress ... • To change the tone of this sentence, I could (change the pitch, volume, speed, etc.) ...	• CCAP • Sound Scripting • Segmental Practice • Suprasegmental Practice
	Examples	
	PK-5 • You said the word **cycle**. It starts with the letter **c**. 6-8 • I can't distinguish between **convection** and **conduction.** 9-12 • The teacher tells a student to verify if the answer is correct by stating, "Those are the products?" The student replies, "Are you telling me or asking me?"	
2(B) recognize elements of the English sound system in newly acquired vocabulary such as long and short vowels, silent letters, and consonant clusters	**Sound System** Teacher Questions • What sound does/do the letter(s) ___ make in the word ___? • What sound does the vowel ___ make in the word ___? • Is ___ a long/short vowel in the word ___? Student Sentence Stems • I hear ___ in the word ___. • The sound I heard was... • The word you said has a ... • ___ has the ___ sound.	• Word Wall • Word Sorts • Songs/Poems/ Rhymes • Systematic Phonics Instruction • Segmental Practice
	Examples	
	PK-12 • The sound I heard was **a short vowel "a".** • The word **change** has a silent **e**. • **Graph** has the "f" sound.	

Sentence Stems and Activities Aligned to
Cross-Curricular Student Expectations
(subsection c)

Listening		
2(C) learn new language structures, expressions, and basic and academic vocabulary heard during classroom instruction and interactions	**Language Structures/Expressions during Interactions** Teacher Question • What new terms did you hear during the lesson? • The following are some examples of question stems commonly used in TEKS. Students should get used to hearing these types of questions during instruction. o How does this affect the...? o Which _____ best models (shows, represents)...? o Which of the following (conditions) most likely caused...? o Which of the following is best classified as _____? o Which of the following best represents...? o Which of these best describes...? o Which characteristic is most...? o Which question could be answered from the data? o What is the best conclusion? o What is the best explanation? o What factors affect...? Student Sentence Stems • I heard the new word/phrase... • One new phrase I used was ... • I heard ___ use the word/phrase ... • An expression I hear in science class is... • A new word/phrase I heard was ... • I can use that word/phrase when ... • I used the word/phrase ___ when I spoke with ... • I used the word/phrase ___ to express the idea that ... **Examples** PK-5 • A new word I heard was **precipitation**. 6-8 • An expression I hear in science class is "**The characteristics associated with**..." 9-12 • I used the word **viral** when I spoke with my doctor.	• Carousel Activity • Creating Words • Oral Scaffolding • Personal Dictionary • Scanning • Self-assessment of Levels of Word Knowledge • Think, Pair, Share, • Vocabulary Self Collection • Vocabulary Alive • Word Sorts
2(D) monitor understanding of spoken language during classroom instruction and interactions and seek clarification as needed	**Clarification during Instruction and Interaction** Teacher Questions/Actions • Do you need more time to think? • Let me repeat the question. • After asking a question, provide ELs sufficient wait-time to formulate a response before asking them to respond. Student Sentence Stems • Can you help me to ...? • I don't understand what/how... • Would you please repeat that? • So you're saying ... • May I please have some more information? • May I have some time to think?	• Inside/Outside Circle • Instructional Conversation • Instructional Scaffolding • Structured Conversation • Think Alouds • Think, Pair, Share • Total Physical Response (TPR)

Sentence Stems and Activities Aligned to
Cross-Curricular Student Expectations
(subsection c)

Listening		
2(E) use visual, contextual, and linguistic support to enhance and confirm understanding of increasingly complex and elaborated spoken language	**Linguistic, Visual, Contextual Support** Teacher Questions • Based on the pictures, what is the lesson going to be about? • How do experiments help you understand science concepts? • How does graphing a table's data help you understand? • How could you represent this pattern with pictures? • What is the problem about? • What graphic organizer would help you...? • What model best demonstrates this concept? • How is this represented in the real world? Student Sentence Stems • The experiment helped me understand... • Using pictures with my observations helps me... • The graphic organizer shows... • The word ___ is on the word wall. • If I want to find out ___, I can ... • I can use ___ to check if I .... • When I hear ___ it tells me ... • Would you please show me on the... (diagram/picture/organizer/notes/etc.)....? • One limitation of the model is...	• Card Sorts • Creating Words • Graphic Organizers • Inside/Outside Circle • Instructional Conversation • Instructional Scaffolding • Multiple Representation Graphic Organizer • Multiple Representation Card Game • Nonlinguistic Representations • Posted Phrases and Stems • Structured Conversation • Think, Pair, Share • Personal Dictionaries
	Examples	
	PK-5 • The pictures help me understand the **life cycle**. 6-8 • The graphic organizer shows the relationship between **elements** and **compounds**. 9-12 • Will you please show me a picture of a **prokaryotic cell**?	
2(F) listen to and derive meaning from a variety of media such as audio tape, video, DVD, and CD ROM to build and reinforce concept and language attainment	**Concept Attainment from a Variety of Media** Teacher Questions • How did the ___ help you understand ___? • How is ___ related to the concept of ___? • What was the ___ about? • How does the website help you understand ___? • How does the graphing calculator help you understand ___? Student Sentence Stems • I notice ... • ___ represents... • I conclude... • It appears... • I heard/saw a ... • ___ can be used in real life to... • The ___ was about... • The video on ___ helps me understand... • The song was about... • I heard/observed ___ which makes me think ... • I think ___ is an example of ___ because... • One characteristic/attribute of ___ that I heard/observed is ...	• Concept Attainment • Concept Mapping • Learning Logs and Journals • Chunking Input • Visual Literacy Frames • Pairs View

Sentence Stems and Activities Aligned to Cross-Curricular Student Expectations
(subsection c)

Listening		
2(F) continued	**Language Attainment from a Variety of Media** Teacher Questions • What words might you hear in the ___? • What new word did you hear/see in the ___? • What do you think ___ means? • Based on the ___, what do you think ___ means? • Student Sentence Stems • ___ means... • I heard/saw the word/phrase ___. • I think the word/ phrase means/does not mean ... • I heard/saw the word/phrase ___. I can use it when... • I heard/saw the word/phrase ___. I might be able to use it when___ because ... • I heard/saw the word/phrase___. I probably would not use it when ___ because ...	
	Examples	
	PK-5 • The **PowerPoint** was about **the water cycle**. • I heard the words **natural** and **manmade**. 6-8 • It appears the **song is about biodiversity**. • I heard the word **human dependence.** 9-12 • The video on **the periodic table** helps me understand **why the table is arranged a certain way**. • The website on **waves** helped me understand **the Doppler effect**.	

2(G) understand the general meaning, main points, and important details of spoken language ranging from situations in which topics, language, and contexts are familiar to unfamiliar	**Meaning in Spoken Language**
	Teacher Questions/Tasks
	• What was the ___ about?
	• What are the instructions?
	• Based on the explanation, how would you...?
	• Based on the clues given, what is the meaning of...?
	• Will you repeat what I just said?
	• What did you understand of what I said?
	• Prompt for elaborated student responses such as:
	   o Explain what ___ just said.
	   o Tell me more about that.
	   o Do you agree with ...? Why/why not?
	   o Why do you think...?
		• Dirty Laundry
		• Graffiti Write
		• Guess Your Corner
		• IEPT
		• Question, Signal, Stem, Share, Assess
		• Reciprocal Teaching
		• Story Telling
		• Structured Conversation
		• Summarization Frames

Sentence Stems and Activities Aligned to
Cross-Curricular Student Expectations
(subsection c)

Listening

2(G) continued	**Student Sentence Stems** • I think ___ means ... • I think ___ means ___ because ... • The ___ is/is not represented by...because • My partner said... • I agree/disagree with ___ because... • ___ said "___." I think it means ... • I heard ___ (the speaker) say ... • I heard you say___. Another way to say that might be... • One thing I heard was ... • One thing ___ (the speaker) said was ... • I have never heard the word/phrase/concept, but I think it means... **Main Point in Spoken Language** Teacher Questions • What steps must you follow to determine the ...? • What is the problem about? • What is the experiment attempting to support? • What is the main point of the article? • What information is irrelevant? Student Sentence Stems • The ___ is... • The ___ describes... • The ___ represents... • It's about... • A generalization is... • I do/don't need to know about... • The experiment is attempting to support the idea that... • Overall our objective is... **Details in Spoken Language** Teacher Questions • What are the attributes/characteristics of...? • From a scale of 1 to 3, how clear were the instructions? • What is step number ___ of the instructions? • What is one important detail you heard? • Why is ___ different from ___? • How are ___ different from ___? Student Sentence Stems • The instructions are... • The first step is... • An attribute I heard is... • My partner said... • My partner said ___ and ___ have... • One characteristic of ___ is... • One important thing I heard (the speaker) say was ... • ___ (The speaker) said ____, which is important because ... • I heard ___ (the speaker) say ___ which supports the idea that ... • I heard that ___ and ___ are different because...	

Sentence Stems and Activities Aligned to Cross-Curricular Student Expectations

(subsection c)

Listening		
2(G) continued	**Examples**	
	PK-5	
	• The teacher holds a watering can (with water) over a model of a house and says, "The water represents one type of precipitation." The student says, "I think **precipitation** means **rain**."	
	• I agree that trees are a **natural resource**.	
	• One type of movement is **sliding**.	
	6-8	
	• I agree with my partner because **runoff of fertilizers can damage the ocean**.	
	• The **average speed** is equal to total distance divided by total time.	
	• The first step is **to use a balance to measure the mass**.	
	9-12	
	• One thing I heard was **waves move differently in different media**.	
	• Overall our objective is **to determine the traits possible in the offspring**.	
	• The instructions are **to create a table for the data and then conduct the experiment**.	
2(H) understand implicit ideas and information in increasingly complex spoken language commensurate with grade-level learning expectations	**Implicit Ideas**	• Instructional Conversation
	Teacher Questions	• Discovery Learning
	• From the ___ what can you conclude?	• Question, Signal, Stem, Share, Assess
	• What is your prediction?	
	• Which procedure could be used for...?	• Reciprocal Teaching
	• Which statement is best supported by...?	• Story Telling
	• Which of the following shows...?	• Structured Conversation
	• Which statement is not true?	• Summarization Frames
	• Which is a reasonable answer?	• Whip Around
	• What can you infer from the ___?	
	• What conclusion can be drawn from...?	
	• Based on the information in the ___, which statement is a valid conclusion?	
	• What might NOT be a valid representation of___?	
	• Which is the best explanation for...?	
	Student Sentence Stems	
	• A valid conclusion is...	
	• The statement is not true because...	
	• I can conclude ___ because...	
	• I can assume ____ because ...	
	• The best explanation is...	
	• My prediction is...	
	• Even though it doesn't say ___, I think ...	
	• Based on ___, I can infer that ...	
	• From the information found in ___ I can infer that ___.	
	• Based on the information I heard in ___, I can conclude...	
	Examples	
	PK-5	
	• My prediction is that more energy will make the ice **melt** faster.	
	6-8	
	• I think the **density** is greater than 1 g/cm³ **because the marble sank in water**.	
	9-12	
	• I can conclude **the reaction is a synthesis reaction because two things are being combined**.	

Sentence Stems and Activities Aligned to
Cross-Curricular Student Expectations
(subsection c)

Listening		

2(I) demonstrate listening comprehension of increasingly complex spoken English by following directions, retelling or summarizing spoken messages, responding to questions and requests, collaborating with peers, and taking notes commensurate with content and grade-level needs	**Following Spoken Directions**
	Teacher Questions/Tasks
	• Who can restate the instructions?
	• What will we do first, second, and finally?
	• Tell your partners what they need to do to complete the task.
	
	Student Sentence Stems
	• The first step is …
	• The next steps are …
	• I know I'm finished because …
	• What you need to do is…
	• The initial step is …
	• The next step(s) in the process is/are
	• I will know I've completed the task successfully when …
	
	Retelling/Summarizing Spoken English
	Teacher Questions/Tasks
	• In your own words, what did ___ just say?
	• Prompt for elaborated student responses such as:
	   o Explain what ___ just said.
	   o Tell me more about that.
	   o Do you agree with …? Why/why not?
	   o Why do you think…?
	
	Student Sentence Stems
	• It's about…
	• The main idea is …
	• First,___. Then,___. Finally,___.
	• I would explain the concept to a friend by …
	• The general idea is…
	
	Responding to Questions/Requests
	Teacher Questions
	• Did anyone think of this problem in a different way?
	• Why did you choose this procedure to answer the question?
	• How does the method relate to the method ___ just explained?
	• Why did you draw ___ to represent a ___?
	• ___ please come and solve the genetics problem ___ on the board.
	
	Student Sentence Stems
	• You asked___. I think …
	• The answer is…
	• I think you're asking …
	• Do you want me to …?
	• I heard you say___, so I need to ….
		• Carousel Activity
		• Creating Words
		• Dirty Laundry
		• Guess Your Corner
		• Framed Oral Recap
		• Keep, Delete, Substitute, Select
		• IEPT
		• Instructional Conversation
		• Mix and Match
		• Note Taking Strategies
		• Outlines
		• Question Answer Relationship (QAR)
		• Question, Signal, Stem, Share, Assess
		• Reader/Writer/Speaker Response Triads
		• Reciprocal Teaching
		• Story Telling
		• Structured Conversation
		• Summarization Frames
		• Tiered Questions
		• Tiered Response Stems
		• W.I.T. Questioning
		• Word MES Questioning

Sentence Stems and Activities Aligned to Cross-Curricular Student Expectations
(subsection c)

Listening		

2(I) continued	**Collaborating With Peers**
	
	Teacher Questions
	• Grouping configurations involving ELLs needs to be predetermined prior to the beginning of instruction. Consider the following when grouping ELLs:
	  o What is the purpose for grouping students?
	  o What are the language proficiency levels and language backgrounds of students?
	  o Does the grouping configuration(s) meet the lesson's objectives?
	
	Student Sentence Stems
	• Can you help me understand ...?
	• Would you please repeat that?
	• What do you think...?
	• Who's responsible for...?
	• Who should ...?
	• My job/part/role is to...
	• So I should ...
	• I'm responsible for ...
	• First, ___. Second, ___. Finally, ___.
	
	Taking Notes
	Teacher Questions
	• What information did you write down?
	• How did you organize the information? Why?
	
	Student Sentence Stems
	• I noted ...
	• The main ideas I wrote down were ...
	• Some details I wrote down were ...
	• I can organize the ideas I wrote by... (making an outline, concept map, Venn diagram, chart, etc.)	

Speaking		
3(A) practice producing sounds of newly acquired vocabulary such as long and short vowels, silent letters, and consonant clusters to pronounce English words in a manner that is increasingly comprehensible	**Producing Sounds** Teacher Questions • What sound does/do the letter(s) ___ make in the word ___? • What sound does the vowel ___ make in the word ___? • Which word has the consonant blend ___? • Is ___ a long/short vowel in the word ___? • How would you pronounce the word ___? Student Sentence Stems • ___ makes the ___ sound. • ___ is pronounced ___. • The word ___ is pronounced ___ because ... • The letter(s) ___ make(s) the ___ sound. • The word ___ begins with the letter... • The word ___ has the long/short vowel ... • The word ___ has a silent ... • The word ___ has the consonant blend ... • The letter ___ in the word ___is long because ... • The ___ is silent in the word ___ because...	• Fluency Workshop • List Stressed Words • Recasting • Segmental Practice • Suprasegmental Practice

Sentence Stems and Activities Aligned to
Cross-Curricular Student Expectations
(subsection c)

Speaking		

3(A) continued	Examples	

	PK-5
	    • The word <u>light</u> has the silent letters <u>gh</u>.
	6-8
	    • The word <u>(teacher/student holds up an index card with the word igneous)</u> is pronounced <u>igneous</u>.
	9-12
	    • The letters <u>PH</u> make an <u>"f"</u> sound in the word <u>photoelectric</u>.	

| 3(B) expand and internalize initial English vocabulary by learning and using high-frequency English words necessary for identifying and describing people, places, and objects, by retelling simple stories and basic information represented or supported by pictures, and by learning and using routine language needed for classroom communication | | • Accountable Conversation Questions
• Conga Line
• Dirty Laundry
• Expert/Novice
• Inside/Outside Circle
• Instructional Conversation
• Numbered Heads Together
• Partner Reading
• Question, Signal, Stem, Share Assess
• Retelling
• Summarization Frames
• Think, Pair, Share
• Vocabulary Alive |

**Description and Simple Story Telling with
High Frequency Words and Visuals**

Examples of high frequency words

About	Best	Face	Little	Place
Above	Better	Few	Long	Point
All	Between	Find	Many	Right
Almost	Big	First	Model	Same
Also	Both	Following	Move	Saw
Always	Change	If	Next	Second
Answer	Different	Important	Not	Small
Around	Down	Large	Often	Time
Because	Enough	Learn	Only	Together
Below	Example	Left	Picture	Which

- My picture is about...
- ___ looks like...
- I can describe ___ with the words...
- The picture(s) show(s) ...
- I know it is a ___ because...
- ___ could be described as___ because ...
- I can draw a ___ to represent a ___.
- A model of a ___ will help me tell you...

**Routine Language for
Classroom Communication**

Teacher Questions/statements
- What gesture do I use to let you know to work in groups?
- If I raise my right hand it means...
- If I say..., it means it is time for...
- If you don't understand what I am saying, you can say...

Student Sentence Stems
- ___ means___.
- Where is/are...?
- Where do I...?
- How do I ...?
- Can you help me ....?
- May I please have some more information?
- May I ask someone for help?
- May I go to...?
- May I...?
- When is it time to ...?

Sentence Stems and Activities Aligned to
Cross-Curricular Student Expectations
(subsection c)

Speaking		

3(C) speak using a variety of grammatical structures, sentence lengths, sentence types, and connecting words with increasing accuracy and ease as more English is acquired	**Speak using a variety of Structures**
	
	Teacher Questions
	• Orally explain...
	   o What are the characteristics of...?
	   o How would you differentiate ___ from ___?
	   o What will happen if...?
	   o What are the similarities between ___ and ___?
	   o Predict what the next ___ will be.
	   o What can you infer from the ___?
	   o What can you conclude from ___?
	
	Student Sentence Stems
	Description
	• A ___ has ___.
	• A ___ is ___, ___, and ___.
	• Additionally, ___ has/have ...
	• ___ is an example of...
	• ___ is an example of....because ...
	
	Sequence
	• First,___. Second,___.
	• First, ___ and then...
	• If the steps in _____ are put in order, _____ would be the first step.
	• _____ has to happen before _____ can happen.
	
	Cause and Effect
	• The ___ is ___ because___.
	• ___ because ___.
	• The cause is ___. The effect is ___.
	• ___ was caused by ___.
	• If ___, then ___.
	• When ___, then...
	• The independent variable is ___, and the dependent variable is___.
	
	Comparison
	• A ___ has ___ but a ___ has ___.
	• ___ and ___ both have...
	• ___ is the same as ___.
	• ___ differs from ___ in that...
	• Although ___ has ___, ___ has ___.
	• ___on the other hand has...
	Predictions
	• The ___ will have...
	• The ___ will be...
	• I predict ___ will...
	• I predict ___ will ___ because...
	• The next picture will be...
	• Due to ___, I think ___ will happen.
	• Consequently, I think...
	Inferences
	• I can infer that...
	• I know ___ because...
	• My conjecture is...
	• From the ___, I can infer...
		• Canned Questions
		• Conga Line
		• Instructional Conversation
		• Experiments/Lab
		• Discovery Learning
		• Fold the Line
		• Numbered Heads Together
		• IEPT
		• Question, Signal, Stem, Share, Assess
		• Reader/Writer/ Speaker Response Triads
		• Signal Words
		• Story Telling
		• Structured Conversation
		• Summarization Frames

Sentence Stems and Activities Aligned to Cross-Curricular Student Expectations
(subsection c)

Speaking		
3(C) continued	*Conclusion* • All ___ are ___. • ___ are ___. • I concluded... • I can conclude that... • If ___, then ___. Therefore...	
	Examples	
	PK-5 **Description** • <u>Magnets</u> are <u>metals</u>. <u>Magnets</u> can pick up paperclips. • <u>Magnets</u> are <u>metals</u> and can pick up paperclips. Sequence • First <u>you add soil</u>. Second <u>you add water</u>. • First <u>you add soil</u> and then <u>add water.</u> 6-8 **Cause and Effect** • The <u>pattern</u> is <u>getting bigger</u>. • The <u>pattern </u>is <u>getting bigger</u> because <u>you add three color tiles each time</u>. **Comparison** • <u>Photosynthesis</u> happens in the <u>chloroplast</u>. <u>Respiration</u> happens in the <u>mitochondria</u>. • <u>Photosynthesis</u> happens in the <u>chloroplast</u> while <u>respiration</u> happens in the <u>mitochondria</u>. **Prediction** • The <u>speed</u> will <u>increase</u>. • I predict <u>the speed will increase</u> because <u>the ramp is higher</u>. 9-12 **Inferences** • I know it will have a stronger/longer <u>reaction</u>. • I know this <u>element will react easily</u> because of its <u>location on the periodic table</u>. **Conclusion** • <u>The offspring might be brown.</u> • I concluded that <u>¾ of the offspring will be brown.</u>	
3(D) speak using grade-level content area vocabulary in context to internalize new English words and build academic language proficiency	**Speak using Science Vocabulary** Teacher Questions The following are some examples of question stems commonly used in TEKS. It is recommended for students to use terms found in these questions during oral discussions. • How does this affect the...? • Which _____ best models (shows, represents)...? • Which of the following (conditions) most likely caused...? • Which of the following is best classified as _____? • Which of the following best represents...? • Which of these best describes...? • Which characteristic is most...? • Which question could be answered using the data? • What is the best conclusion? • What is the best explanation? • What factors affect...? • Which ___ best represents ___? • Which graph best fits the ___? • Which ___ can be used to determine ___?	• Content Specific Stems • Creating Analogies • Creating Words • Dirty Laundry • Instructional Conversation • Mix and Match • Self-assessment of Levels of Word Knowledge • Structured Conversation • Question, Signal, Stem, Share, Assess • Reciprocal Teaching

Sentence Stems and Activities Aligned to Cross-Curricular Student Expectations
(subsection c)

Speaking				
3(D) continued	**Student Sentence Stems** • This affects the ____ because ____. • _____ best models... • This was most likely caused by... • This is best classified as... • _____ represents this concept the best because... • The data shows that... • The best piece of equipment to use is... • ____ is the best explanation of ... • The most important factors are... • Factors that are unimportant include... • I concluded that... • ____ can be used to determine...			
	Examples of Science Vocabulary			

PK-5

Adaptations	Freezing	Liquid	Nonrenewable	Renewable
Animals	Gas	Living	Objects	Resources
Behavior	Growth	Magnet	Offspring	Safety
Color	Heat	Man made	Orbit	Shape
Ecosystem	Interactions	Mass	Organism	Size
Energy	Interdependent	Matter	Patterns	Soil
Environment	Investigation	Melting	Physical	Solid
Food chain	Landform	Motion	Plants	Sound
Food web	Life cycle	Natural	Predict	Temperature
Force	Light	Nonliving	Property	Weather

6-8

Atomic	Convection	Heterotroph	Molecular	Precipitate
Autotroph	Decay	Hypotheses	Natural Selection	Prokaryote
Catastrophe	Density	Inherit	Nonmetals	Radiant
Cell	Domain	Kinetic Energy	Nucleus	Radiation
Chemical reaction	Elements	Kingdom	Organelle	Solar System
Classify	Eukaryote	Luster	Organic	Succession
Community	Experiment	Malleability	Periodic Table	Symbols
Compounds	Function	Metalloids	Plate Tectonics	Taxonomy
Conduction	Geotropism	Metals	Population	Thermal Energy
Conductivity	Gravity	Mixtures	Potential Energy	Variation

9-12

Acceleration	Endothermic	Homeostasis	Precision	Stoichiometry
Acid	Equipment	Insulator	Product	Structure
Base	Evidence	Ionic	Quantitative	Substances
Conclusion	Evolution	Law	Radioactive	Transcription
Conductor	Exothermic	Magnitude	Reactant	Transfer
Conservation	Fission	Momentum	Replication	Transformation
Corrosive	Flammable	Parallel circuit	RNA	Translation
Covalent	Formula	Pattern	Series circuit	Trend
Design	Function	pH	Solute	Virus
DNA	Fusion	Poison	Speed	Wave

Sentence Stems and Activities Aligned to Cross-Curricular Student Expectations
(subsection c)

Speaking		

3(E) share information in cooperative learning interactions	**Share in Cooperative Interactions**
	Teacher Questions
	• Grouping configurations involving ELLs needs to be predetermined prior to the beginning of instruction. Consider the following when grouping ELLs:
	  o What is the purpose for grouping students?
	  o What are the language proficiency levels and language backgrounds of students?
	  o Does the grouping configuration(s) meet the lesson's objectives?
	
	Student Sentence Stems
	• An idea is...
	• My guess is...
	• I think...
	• A characteristic is...
	• First,... Second,... Finally,...
	• The way I would solve the problem is...
	• The ___ can be represented with...
	• What I know about ___ is...
	• My suggestion would be ___ because...
	• I agree/disagree that...because...
	• In my opinion, the answer is reasonable because
	• To solve the problem, we can...
	• Is your answer reasonable? How do you know?
		• Carousel Activity
		• Conga Line
		• Fold the Line
		• Inside Outside Circle
		• Instructional Conversation
		• Structured Conversation
		• Question, Signal, Stem, Share, Assess
		• Peer Editing
		• Pairs View
		• Partner Reading
		• Interview Grids

3(F) ask and give information ranging from using a very limited bank of high-frequency, high-need, concrete vocabulary, including key words and expressions needed for basic communication in academic and social contexts, to using abstract and content-based vocabulary during extended speaking assignments	**Ask and Give Information** Teacher Questions/Requests • Write two questions for your partner to answer. • What question do you have about the lesson? • What is your answer to the question? • Explain your reasoning to a partner. • Explain to your partner why you agree/disagree with his/her answer? **NOTE:** How, what, why, where, and when are high frequency words. Student Sentence Stems | Ask for Information	Give Information
---	---
How do you ...?	First you ... then...
What is...?	___ is ...
What did you notice about/in...?	I noticed ...
What are the characteristic of ...?	One characteristic of ___ is...
What do you think caused ...?	I think ___ caused ___ because...
When do you...?	You ___ when....
Where do you place...?	You ___ the ___ in the...
Why did you use...?	I used the ___ because...		• Instructional Conversation • Interview Grids • Mix and Match • Question, Signal, Stem, Share, Assess • Structured Conversation • Think, Pair, Share

Sentence Stems and Activities Aligned to
Cross Curricular Student Expectations
(subsection c)

Speaking		
3(G) express opinions, ideas, and feelings ranging from communicating single words and short phrases to participating in extended discussions on a variety of social and grade-appropriate academic topics	**Express Opinions, Ideas, and Feelings** Teacher Questions • What do you think about...? • What is your position on...? • Is the answer reasonable? Why? • How did you reach that solution/conclusion? • Will you please elaborate on your response? • Do you agree/disagree with...? Why? • Is there another solution to this problem? Please explain. • Is there a counter example to ....? State the counter example. • Tell me more about... • What else can you tell me about...? • Which model do you think is the strongest? Student Sentence Stems • I believe ___. • My position is ___. • I think ___. • I think ___ because... • In addition, I think... • I predict... • A solution is.... • I solved the problem by... • The problem can be solved by... • Another solution is ___ because... • The answer is ___. • The answer is ___ because... • The answer is/isn't reasonable because... • I agree/disagree because... • I agree/disagree with ___ because... • ___ represents a ___. • ___ represents a ___ because... • _____ is the strongest model because...	• Anticipation Chat • Conga Line • Instructional Conversation • Question, Signal, Stem, Share, Assess • Reciprocal Teaching • Structured Conversation • Think, Pair, Share • W.I.T. Questioning
	Examples	
	PK-5 • I think the next one will be a full moon. • I think the **next picture will be of a full moon** because **the one before it is of a waxing gibbous**. **6-8** • **Hollow bones in birds** represent an **adaptation**. • **Hollow bones in birds** represent an **adaptation** because **they are lightweight which helps with flight**. **9-12** • The best piece of equipment to use is a graduated cylinder. • I agree because **graduated cylinders are more accurate than beakers**.	

Sentence Stems and Activities Aligned to Cross-Curricular Student Expectations
(subsection c)

Speaking		
3(H) narrate, describe, and explain with increasing specificity and detail as more English is acquired	**Narrate, Describe, and Explain with Increasing Detail** Teacher Questions • How would you describe...? • In your own words, explain why... • Why did ___ happen? • What else can you say about...? • Will you please restate what ___ said? • Explain how you reached that conclusion. Student Sentence Stems • This is a ... • The solution is... • The solution is... because... • ___ best represents ___. • ___ best represents ___ because... • ___ is about... • The most important attribute is... • ___ is the most important attribute because... • It's important to remember... • Initially,___. Then,___ Ultimately,___. • First,___. Then,___. Finally,___. • Evidence for my conclusion includes...	• Creating Words • Instructional Conversation • Numbered Heads Together • Question, Signal, Stem, Share, Assess • Roundtable • Story Telling • Structured Conversation • Summarization Frames
	Examples	
	PK-5 • This is a **plant**. • This is a **plant** and it has a **stem** and **leaves**. 6-8 • The density is **.5 g/ml**. • The density is .**5g/ml** because **a mass of 4 grams divided by a volume of 8 ml is .5 g/ml**. 9-12 • The most important process is **replication**. • The most important process is **DNA replication** because **it ensures new cells contain a full set of genetic instructions**.	
3(I) adapt spoken language appropriately for formal and informal purposes	**Formal and Informal Spoken English** • ___ means ___. • ___ could be a ___ but in science ___ means ___. • The object... • Another word for ___ is ___. • At school we say ___ instead of... • I would explain the pattern/table/graph/picture to a friend by ... • In science we use the word/phrase ... to ... • I would describe ___ to someone outside of school by ... • I would describe ___ using science language by ...	• Chat Room • Expert/Novice • Mix and Match • Oral Scaffolding • Radio Talk Show • Sentence Sort • Word Sorts
	Examples	
	PK-5 • The rock was **worn away**. • The rock was **weathered**. 6-8 • Another word for **passed down** is **inherited**. • At school, we say **function** instead of **purpose.** 9-12 • In biology we use the word **homeostasis** to describe **how organisms maintain a stable internal environment.**	

Sentence Stems and Activities Aligned to Cross-Curricular Student Expectations
(subsection c)

Speaking		
3(J) respond orally to information presented in a wide variety of print, electronic, audio, and visual media to build and reinforce concept and language attainment	**Concept Attainment from a Variety of Media** Teacher Questions • How did the ___ help you understand ___? • How is ___ related to the concept of ___? • What was the ___ about? • How does the animation help you understand ___? • How does the investigation help you understand ___? Student Sentence Stems • I notice … • ___ represents… • I concluded… • It appears… • I heard/saw a … • ___ can be used in the real life to… • The ___ was about… • The video on ___ helps me understand… • The song was about… • I heard/observed ___ which makes me think … • I think ___ is an example of ___ because… • One characteristic/attribute of ____ that I heard/observed is … **Language Attainment from a Variety of Media** Teacher Questions • What words might you hear in the ___? • What new word did you hear/see in the ___? • What do you think ___ means? • Based on the ___, what do you think ___ means? • How does the computer program help you understand the meaning of…? • What did they mean by…? • Why did they use the word ___ to describe ___? Student Sentence Stems • ___ means… • I think the word means/does not mean … • I see/hear… • The word ___ was used… • I noticed the word ___ is pronounced… • I heard/saw the word(s) ___. • I heard/saw the word ___. I can use it when… • Words that were unfamiliar are ___, ___ and ___.	• Chunking Input • Concept Attainment • Concept Definition Map • Learning Logs and Journals • Pairs View • Visual Literacy Frames
	Examples	
	PK-5 • The **PowerPoint** was about **safety rules and equipment**. • I heard the words **safety goggles.** 6-8 • It appears **that the seasons are caused by the tilt of the Earth on its axis**. • I noticed the word **eukaryotic** is pronounced **eukaryotic**. 9-12 • The video on **chromosomal analysis** helps me understand **how we study the genomes of organisms**. • **The arrow (→) in a chemical equation** means **yields or produces.**	

Sentence Stems and Activities Aligned to Cross-Curricular Student Expectations
(subsection c)

Reading		
4(A) learn relationships between sounds and letters of the English language and decode (sound out) words using a combination of skills such as recognizing sound-letter relationships and identifying cognates, affixes, roots, and base words	**Decoding** Teacher Questions • What sound does/do the letter(s) ___ make in the word ___? • What sound does/do the vowel(s) ___ make in the word ___? • Is ___ a long/short vowel in the word ___? Student Sentence Stems • The letter(s) ___ make(s) the ___ sound... • The word ___ has the long/short vowel ... • The word ___ has a silent ... • The word ___ has the consonant blend ... • The letter ___ in the word ___is long because ... • The ___ is silent in the word ___ because... • The word ___ is pronounced ___ because ... **Cognates** Teacher Questions • What is a cognate? • What is the cognate of the word...? • What are some examples of false cognates? Student Sentence Stems • The word ___ helps me spell the word ___. • The word ___ sounds like ___ in my language and means ... • The word ___ sounds like___ in my language, but does NOT mean...	• Direct Teaching of Affixes • Direct Teaching of Cognates • Direct Teaching of Roots • Self-assessment of Levels of Word Knowledge • Word Generation • Word Sorts • Word Study Books • Word Walls

Examples of Science Cognates

Characteristics Características	Classify Clasificar	Conclusions Conclusiones	Cycle Ciclo	Diagram Diagrama
Energy Energía	Evidence Evidencia	Experiment Experimento	Group Grupo	Laboratory Laboratorio
Matter Materia	Observations Observaciones	Parts Partes	Science Ciencia	Systems Sistemas

Affixes, Roots, and Base words
Teacher Questions
- What does the prefix/suffix ___ mean?
- What does the root word ___ mean?
- How does knowing the meaning of ___ help you figure out what ___ means?

Student Sentence Stems
- ___ means ___.
- ___ means ___ because...
- The word___ has the prefix/suffix/root ___ which means...
- The base word is...
- The base word in the word ___ is...
- Some other words with this prefix/suffix/root are ...
- This word probably means ___ because...

Examples of Roots, Base Words, Prefixes, and Suffixes used in Science

Root	Base Word	Prefix	Suffix
Anim	Atom	In-	-ic/-ical
Aqua	Nature	Multi-	-ocity
Endo	Observe	Pro-	-troph

Sentence Stems and Activities Aligned to
Cross-Curricular Student Expectations
(subsection c)

Reading		

4(B) recognize directionality of English reading such as left to right and top to bottom	**Directionality of English Text**
	
	Teacher Questions
	• What is the directionality of script of the ___ language?
	    o Arabic (Right to Left)
	    o English (Left to Right)
	    o Korean (Left to Right or Top to Bottom)
	    o Mandarin (Left to Right or Top to Bottom)
	    o Russian (Left to Right)
	    o Urdu (Right to Left)
	
	Student Sentence Stems
	• In English, words go … *(students can use gestures to indicate directionality)*
	• In ____ (Chinese/Arabic/Hebrew, etc.) words go…, but in English words go…
	• In___ (Spanish/French/Russian, etc.) words go…., and in English words also go…
		• Total Physical Response (TPR)
		• Directionality Sort

4(C) develop basic sight vocabulary, derive meaning of environmental print, and comprehend English vocabulary and language structures used routinely in written classroom materials	**Sight Vocabulary/** Teacher Questions: • How many times did you use/read/hear the sight word ___? Examples of sight vocabulary words <table><tr><td>A</td><td>Be</td><td>Fast</td><td>May</td><td>To</td></tr><tr><td>And</td><td>Call</td><td>Give</td><td>Some</td><td>Use</td></tr><tr><td>All</td><td>Cut</td><td>Going</td><td>The</td><td>We</td></tr><tr><td>Are</td><td>Every</td><td>Had</td><td>Think</td><td>You</td></tr></table> Student Sentence Stems • I know… • ___ means… • I used/read/heard the word ___. • What are sight words? **Environmental Print** Teacher Questions • What is environmental print? • How does environmental print help students comprehend vocabulary? • What should be labeled in the classroom? • Students show understanding of environmental print through actions with gestures or use simple phrases. Student Sentence Stems • This is a ___. • The symbol says/means… • This sign says ____. It tells me… • Labeling things in the room helps me understand ____ because… Examples PK-12 Student points to posted illustration and says… • This is a **cycle**. • The symbol means **energy is added**. • That is a **cloud**.	• Expert/Novice • Oral Scaffolding • Total Physical Response (TPR)

Sentence Stems and Activities Aligned to
Cross-Curricular Student Expectations
(subsection c)

Reading		
4(D) use pre-reading supports such as graphic organizers, illustrations, and pretaught topic-related vocabulary and other prereading activities to enhance comprehension of written text	**Pre Reading Supports** Teacher Questions • What do you know about...? • What do you remember about...? • What is an example of a...? • What is a ...? • What is a type of ...? • What experience have you had with...? • What have you learned about...? • Close your eyes and think of ___. What do you see? • What comes to mind when you think of...? • What does the picture/word/phrase remind you of? • What does ___ mean to you? • How can ___ be represented? • How have you used...? • What do you think the word ___ means? • What do you know about...? What do you want to learn about...? • Is ___ true or false? • What words in the instructions are unfamiliar to you? • Think about a time when you... Student Sentence Stems • I know.... • I remember... • A ___ is... • A type of ___ is... • I learned... • I see... • I have used ___ to... • An example of a ___ is... • The pictures are about ... • The statement is (true/false). • I think ___ means... • I think this ___ is about ... • A time I used ___ was when... • An experience I have had with ___ is... • A ___ can be represented with a... • The diagram/table/graph helps me... • The graphic organizer is about... • The organizer shows me that ___ is significant because ... • The diagram/table/graph tells me the ___ is about ... • The strategy that will help me understand these instructions the best is probably.... *(note taking, scanning, surveying key text features such as bold words, illustrations and headings, using the wordlist, etc.)*	• Advance Organizers • Anticipation Guides • Backwards Book Walk • Comprehension Strategies • DRTA • Scanning • SQP2RS • Visuals • Word Walls

Sentence Stems and Activities Aligned to Cross-Curricular Student Expectations
(subsection c)

Reading		
4(D) continued	**Examples**	
	PK-5	
	• I know <u>**electricity**</u> travels through a circuit.	
	• I have used <u>**a balance**</u> to measure mass.	
	• I learned <u>**canyons**</u> are like big ditches.	
	6-8	
	• An example of a <u>**Protist**</u> is an amoeba.	
	• I think <u>**reproduction**</u> means to have offspring.	
	• A <u>**molecule**</u> can be represented with a <u>**chemical formula**</u>.	
	9-12	
	• The picture of <u>**DNA replicating**</u> reminds me of <u>**a zipper unzipping**</u>.	
	• I remember <u>**acids**</u> have a pH less than 7.	
	• A type of <u>**wave**</u> is a transverse wave.	

4(E) read linguistically accommodated content area material with a decreasing need for linguistic accommodations as more English is learned	**Use of Linguistically Accommodated Material**
	Teacher Questions
	• During lesson preparation, teachers make considerations on how to adapt reading materials based on ELLs' language proficiency levels, literacy levels in the native and target language, and educational background. When planning, consider the following questions:
	    o How can the reading material be stated in simpler terms without diminishing the rigor of the science concept?
	    o What picture(s)/table/graph/manipulative/graphic organizer can be used to help students understand the reading material?
	    o What irrelevant information can be deleted from the problem?
	
	Student Sentence Stems
	• ___ helped me to understand/write/say … (*native language summary, native language wordlist, picture dictionary, outline, simplified English text, sentence starters, etc.*)
	• The outline helped me because…
	• The problem is about…
		• Adapted Text
		• Comprehension Strategies
		• Graphic Organizers
		• Insert Method
		• Margin Notes
		• Native Language Texts
		• Outlines
		• Related Literature
		• SQP2RS
		• Taped Text

	Examples	
	<u>**Adapted Text**</u> • Animals are multicellular, heterotrophs with nuclei. What are some examples of animals? Compared to: • Animals have many cells. Animals are heterotrophs. This means they consume or eat other organisms for energy. The cells of animals have nuclei. Dogs and fish are both animals. What are two other examples of animals?	

Sentence Stems and Activities Aligned to Cross-Curricular Student Expectations

(subsection c)

Reading		
4(F) use visual and contextual support and support from peers and teachers to read grade-appropriate content area text, to enhance and confirm understanding, to develop vocabulary, to grasp language structures, and to tap background knowledge needed to comprehend increasingly challenging language	**Using Visual/Contextual Support to Understand Text** Teacher Questions • Based on the picture(s)/table/graph/ graphic organizer, what is the problem/text about? • How do manipulatives help you understand the reading materials? • How could you solve this problem by using manipulatives/visualization/illustrations/diagrams? • What is the problem situation about? Student Sentence Stems *Reading* • The illustrations tell me this word problem/reading material is about … • The diagram/graph/pattern tells me the text is about … • The organizer tells me that I should pay attention to … • The organizer shows me that ___ is significant because … *Confirming understanding* • I raise my hand when… • I don't understand… • I can check if I understand what I'm reading by… • The strategy that will help me to understand this text the best is probably…. *(note taking, scanning, surveying key text features, drawing, guess and check, write an equation, make a table, etc.)* because… *Developing Vocabulary and Background Knowledge* • I use the word wall/wordlist while I read because… • When I come across an unfamiliar word or phrase, I can … *Grasp of Language Structures* • When I see ___ in a problem, it tells me…. • I noticed a lot of ____ in the problem/reading material. It probably means… **Using Teacher/Peer Support to Understand Text** *Reading* • What is the problem/reading material about? • What does ___ mean? • Will you read ___ for me? • Would you please show me on the (diagram/picture/organizer /notes/etc.)…? *Confirming understanding* • It seems like ___. Is that right? • Can you help me understand…? • Can I please have some more information about …? • Where can I find out how to …? • Can I ask someone for help with …? *Developing Vocabulary and Background* • Will you please explain what ___ means? • Does ___ also mean …? • Why does the text have …? *Grasp of Language Structures* • One word/expression that I saw was… • What does the word/expression ____ mean? • Why is there a lot of ____ in the text?	• Anticipation Chat • Comprehension Strategies • DRTA • Graphic Organizers • Imrov. Read Aloud • Insert Method • Nonlinguistic Representations • QtA • Question, Signal, Stem, Share, Assess • Scanning • SQP2RS

Sentence Stems and Activities Aligned to Cross-Curricular Student Expectations
(subsection c)

Reading		

4(G) demonstrate comprehension of increasingly complex English by participating in shared reading, retelling or summarizing material, responding to questions, and taking notes commensurate with content area and grade level needs	**Shared Reading**
	Teacher Questions
	• I will read the problem first. Who wants to re-read the problem?
	• I will read the first step. Who wants to re-read the first step?
	• What does ___ mean?
	• What are the most important details?
	• Why is the table/picture/graph important to understand the word problem/reading material?
	• Let's read the instructions together.
	
	Student Sentence Stems
	• The instructions say...
	• I will read ...
	• I'm responsible for ...
	• The table/picture/graph says...
	• The table/picture/graph is important because...
	• What does the word ___ mean?
	• My job/part/role is to...
	• Can you help me understand ...?
	• Will you please read the step again?
	• Would you please repeat that again?
	
	Retelling/Summarizing
	Teacher Questions/Tasks
	• In your own words, what is the word problem/reading material about?
	• Prompt for elaborated student responses such as:
	  o Explain what ___ just said.
	  o Tell me more about that.
	  o Do you agree with ...? Why/why not?
	  o Why do you think...?
	
	Student Sentence Stems
	• It's about...
	• The experiment is about...
	• The instructions are asking me to...
	• First,...Then,...Finally,...
	• I would explain ___ to a friend by ...
	• Some ideas that could help me solve the problem include...
	
	Responding to Questions/Requests
	Teacher Questions
	• Did anyone think of this problem in a different way?
	• Why did you choose that method?
	• How does the method relate to the method ___ just explained?
	• Why did you draw ___ to represent a ___?
	• ___ please come and solve problem number ___ on the board.
	
	Student Sentence Stems
	• The answer is...
	• I think you're asking ...
	• Do you want me to ...?
	• I heard you say___, so I need to ....
		• Carousel Activity
		• Cornell Notes
		• Guess Your Corner
		• Guided Notes
		• Keep, Delete, Substitute
		• Mix and Match
		• Numbered Heads Together
		• Question, Signal, Stem, Share, Assess
		• Reciprocal Teaching
		• Polya's Problem Solving Method
		• Story Telling
		• Structured Conversation
		• Summarization Frames

Sentence Stems and Activities Aligned to Cross-Curricular Student Expectations
(subsection c)

Reading		
4(G) continued	**Taking Notes** Teacher Questions • What information did you write down? • How did you organize the information? Why? Student Sentence Stems • I noted … • I can draw a… • I can act it out by… • The main ideas I wrote down were … • Some details I wrote down were … • I can organize the ideas I wrote by… (making an outline, concept map, Venn diagram, chart, etc.)	
4(H) read silently with increasing ease and comprehension for longer periods	**Read Silently with Increasing Comprehension** Teacher Questions • What are the instructions asking you to do/find? • What are some important details about the reading? • What is the irrelevant information in the problem? Student Sentence Stems • I need to… • I read about … • I understood/didn't understand… • The word problem/reading material/textbook says… • I think I need to… • ___ is irrelevant information because… **Examples** PK-5 • I need to **draw and label a picture of a plant**. 6-8 • I didn't understand **the word coefficients in the explanation**. 9-12 • I think I need to **find the acceleration of the car**.	• Adapted Text • Double Entry Journals • Idea Bookmarks • Structured Conversation
4(I) demonstrate English comprehension and expand reading skills by employing basic reading skills such as demonstrating understanding of supporting ideas and details in text and graphic sources, summarizing text, and distinguishing main ideas from details commensurate with content area needs	**Supporting Ideas and Details** **Graphic Sources** Teacher Questions • What is the important information in the instructions? • What information is needed to solve the problem? • Who…? What…? When…? How…? Which…? Student Sentence Stems • ___ is important. • I highlighted/circled ___, ___, and ___. • ___ is not needed to solve the problem. • The illustrations tell me this problem/reading material is about.. • This illustration/chart/diagram shows … • This illustration/diagram/graph/chart is significant because …	• Comprehension Strategies • DRTA • Graphic Organizers • Learning Logs • Nonlinguistic Representation • Numbered Heads Together • Polya's Problem Solving Method • Question, Signal, Stem, Share, Assess • QtA

Sentence Stems and Activities Aligned to Cross-Curricular Student Expectations

(subsection c)

Reading		
4(I) continued	**Summarizing** Teacher Questions • What steps will you follow to solve the word problem? • What is the reading material/problem about? • How can we summarize the explanation? Student Sentence Stems • This is about ... • I need to solve for... • I think I need to... **Distinguishing Main Ideas and Details** Teacher Questions • What is the main idea of the word problem? • What are the important facts that will help understand the concept? Student Sentence Stems • The difference between ___ and ___ is... • The main idea of this problem is ... • One detail that is important to understand the concept is ... • First, I need to ___. Second, I need to ___.	• Polya's Problem Solving Method • Scanning • SQP2RS • Structured Conversation • Summarization Frames
	Examples	
	Word Problem Lauren and David noticed that some of the plants in the class garden grow faster than others. They decide to conduct an experiment by planting seeds in 10 pots. Two seeds were planted in each pot. For fun, they decide to put half the pots in a closet to see if they grow in the dark. They will water each plant with 50mL of water each day. Every other day they will measure the height of each plant using a string they marked in centimeters. What parts of the experiment described follow proper experimental design, and which would you change? **Main Idea** • What parts of the experiment described follow proper experimental design and which would you change? **Supporting Details** • Used 2 seeds only of each type • Put half the plants in the dark • Gave each plant the same amount of water each day • Used a string marked in centimeters	
4(J) demonstrate English comprehension and expand reading skills by employing inferential skills such as predicting, making connections between ideas, drawing inferences and conclusions from text and graphic sources, and finding supporting text evidence commensurate with content area needs	**Predicting** Teacher Questions • Based on what you read, what do you think will happen...? • What will happen if...? • What might happen next...? • Do you predict the answer will be ___ or ___? Student Sentence Stems • I think... • I predict ___ will happen next because... • Based on the information in the problem/graph/table, it seems that ___ will probably....	• Comprehension Strategies • DRTA • Graphic Organizers • Nonlinguistic Representations • Scanning • Summarization Frames • SQP2RS

Sentence Stems and Activities Aligned to
Cross-Curricular Student Expectations
(subsection c)

Reading		
4(J) continued	**Making Connections Between Ideas** Teacher Questions • How does ___ help you understand ___? • What is the relationship between ___ and ___? • How else can you represent the ___? • Which is the best model for...? • How does ___ remind you of...? Student Sentence Stems • ___ reminds me of ... • ___ is similar to ... • ___ is different from ... • The relationship between ___ and ___ is... • ___ relates to what happened when ___ because... • ___ is the result of __ because... • If ___, then... **Drawing Inferences and Conclusions** Teacher Questions • What can you infer/conclude from the...? • What does infer mean? Student Sentence Stems • I can infer that ... • I can assume ____ because ... • Even though it doesn't say ___, I think ... • Based on ___, I can conclude that ... • From the information found in ___, I can infer that ___ because ... **Finding Supporting Text Evidence** Teacher Questions • Based on what information can you...? • What information supports your conclusion? • What evidence supports your conclusions? • What information supported your prediction? • How did the graph/picture/table/manipulative help you...? Student Sentence Stems • The ___ helped me because... • I think___ because ... • ____ supports the idea that ... • I think ___ is evidence that ... • ___ corroborates the idea that ... • Based on the information found in ____, I can conclude that __ because...	• Question, Signal, Stem, Share, Assess • Structured Conversation • Learning Logs and Journals • QtA • Prediction Café • Structured Academic Controversy

Sentence Stems and Activities Aligned to Cross-Curricular Student Expectations
(subsection c)

Reading		
4(K) demonstrate English comprehension and expand reading skills by employing analytical skills such as evaluating written information and performing critical analyses commensurate with content area and grade-level needs	**Evaluating Written Information/Performing Critical Analysis** Teacher Questions <ul><li>How can you determine if your partner's explanation is reasonable?</li><li>What evidence is there to support your conclusion?</li><li>Based on what information did you reach that conclusion?</li><li>How did you organize the information?</li></ul> Student Sentence Stems <ul><li>One conclusion is…</li><li>A nonexample is…</li><li>I can generalize that…</li><li>The best way to represent this concept is___ because…</li><li>I tried ___ but it didn't work because…</li><li>The evidence that supports the conclusion is…</li><li>The solution is/isn't reasonable because…</li><li>Your solution is reasonable/not reasonable because…</li><li>I agree/disagree with the explanation because…</li><li>The conclusions are logical because…</li><li>The procedure was accomplished by…</li><li>My partner's explanation was organized/not organized clearly because…</li></ul>	<ul><li>Book Reviews</li><li>Comprehension Strategies</li><li>Double Entry Journals</li><li>DRTA</li><li>Graphic Organizers</li><li>Learning Logs and Journals</li><li>Nonlinguistic Representations</li><li>Polya's Problem Solving Method</li><li>QtA</li><li>Question, Signal, Stem, Share, Assess</li><li>Scanning</li><li>SQP2RS</li><li>Structured Academic Controversy</li><li>Structured Conversation</li><li>Summarization Frames</li></ul>

Sentence Stems and Activities Aligned to Cross-curricular Student Expectations
(subsection c)

Writing		
5(A) learn relationships between sounds and letters of the English language to represent sounds when writing in English	**Letter/Sound Relationship in Writing** Teacher Questions <ul><li>What sound does/do the letter(s) ___ make in the word ___?</li><li>What sound does the vowel ___ make in the word ___?</li><li>Which word has the consonant blend ___?</li><li>Is ___ a long/short vowel in the word ___?</li><li>How would you write the word ___?</li></ul>Student Sentence Stems <ul><li>___ makes ___ sound.</li><li>___ is pronounced ___. Therefore, it is spelled...</li><li>The letter(s) ___ make(s) the ___ sound.</li><li>The word ___ begins with the letter...</li><li>The word ___ has the long/short vowel ...</li><li>The word ___ has a silent ...</li><li>The word ___ has the consonant blend ...</li><li>The letter ___ in the word ___is long because ...</li><li>The ___ is silent in the word ___ because...</li><li>The word ___ is pronounced ___ because ...</li></ul>	<ul><li>Homophone/ Homograph Sort</li><li>Word Sorts</li><li>Word Study Books</li><li>Word Walls</li></ul>
	Examples	
	PK-5 <ul><li>The word **light** has the silent letters **gh**.</li></ul>6-8 <ul><li>The word **(teacher/student holds up an index card with the word metalloids)** is pronounced **metalloids**.</li></ul>9-12 <ul><li>The letters **ph** make an **"f"** sound in the word **photosynthesis**.</li></ul>	
5(B) write using newly acquired basic vocabulary and content-based grade-level vocabulary	**Write using New Vocabulary** Teacher Questions The following are some examples of question stems commonly used in TEKS. It is recommended for students to use terms found in these questions during writing exercises. <ul><li>How does this affect the...?</li><li>Which _____ best models (shows, represents)...?</li><li>Which of the following (conditions) most likely caused...?</li><li>Which of the following is best classified as _____?</li><li>Which of the following best represents...?</li><li>Which of these best describes...?</li><li>Which characteristic is most...?</li><li>Which question could be answered from the data?</li><li>What is the best conclusion?</li><li>What is the best explanation?</li><li>What factors affect...?</li><li>Which ___ best represents ___?</li><li>Which graph best fits the ___?</li><li>Which ___ can be used to determine ___?</li></ul>	<ul><li>Choose the Words</li><li>Cloze Sentences</li><li>Dialogue Journal</li><li>Dirty Laundry</li><li>Double Entry Journals</li><li>Field Notes</li><li>Graffiti Write</li><li>Learning Logs and Journals</li><li>Read, Write, Pair, Share</li><li>Roundtable</li><li>Self-assessment of Levels of Word Knowledge</li><li>Think, Pair, Share</li><li>Word Sort</li><li>Word Walls</li><li>Ticket Out</li></ul>

Sentence Stems and Activities Aligned to
Cross-Curricular Student Expectations
(subsection c)

Writing		
5(B) continued	**Student Sentence Stems** • ___ best represents.___. • ___ could be used to___. • ___ is for ___. • A common characteristic between ___ and ___ is... • ___ has exactly ___. • If ___, then ___. • ___ best fits ___. • ___ is the closest to ___. • ___ appears to be ___. • ___ describes ___. • The best explanation is... • The effect is... • The opposite of ___ is... • ___ can be used to determine ___. • The ___ that is always true is... • If the pattern continues, the next picture will be... • At this rate, it will take...	
	Examples	
	• For examples of high frequency words, content vocabulary, and sight words go to student expectations 3(B), 3(D), and 4(C).	
5(C) spell familiar English words with increasing accuracy, and employ English spelling patterns and rules with increasing accuracy as more English is acquired	**English Spelling Patterns and Rules** Teacher Questions • How is the word ___ spelled? • Does the word ___ start with ___ or ___? • What does the word ___ start/end with? • Is the word spelled with the vowel ___ or ___? • Did you write the word ___ with the vowel/letter ___ or ___? • What are words students commonly misspell? Student Sentence Stems • ___ is spelled ... • ___ begins/ends with the letter ... • I spelled the word ___ with a ___. • In this set of words I notice ... • These words are all similar because ... • The spelling rule that applies to this word is ___ because ... • This word is spelled correctly/incorrectly because ... • I can check my spelling by ... • Is this the correct spelling for...? • Is ___ spelled with a ___ or ___? • How do you spell...? • Will you please check the spelling of the word ____?	• Homophone/ Homograph Sort • Peer Editing • Personal Spelling Guide • Word Analysis • Word Sorts • Word Walls

Sentence Stems and Activities Aligned to Cross-Curricular Student Expectations
(subsection c)

Writing		
5(D) edit writing for standard grammar and usage, including subject-verb agreement, pronoun agreement, and appropriate verb tenses commensurate with grade-level expectations as more English is acquired	**Grammar and Usage** Teacher Questions • What are some common editing symbols? • How can you use editing symbols to help your classmate correct grammatical mistakes? • Did you use the correct verb agreement, pronoun agreement or verb tense in your sentence? How do you know? • Which verb would you use to...? • When do you use __ instead of ___? Student Sentence Stems • The subject ___ agrees/disagrees with the verb___ because... • The pronoun ___ agrees/disagrees with ___ because... • The present/past/future/conditional tense is appropriate/inappropriate in this sentence because ...	• Contextualized Grammar Instruction • Daily Oral Language • Oral Scaffolding • Peer Editing • Reciprocal Teaching • Sentence Mark Up • Sentence Sort
	Example	
	PK-5 • **The temperatures are** 37°C. **vs. The temperature is** 37°C . • Manuel said **he observe** the fish. **vs.** Manuel said **he observed** the fish. 6-8 • The **cell are** all plant cells. **vs.** The **cells** are all plant cells. 9-12 • The **nucleuses** can be seen. **vs.** The **nuclei** can be seen.	
5(E) employ increasingly complex grammatical structures in content area writing commensurate with grade-level expectations, such as: (i) using correct verbs, tenses, and pronouns/ antecedents; (ii) using possessive case (apostrophe s) correctly; and (iii) using negatives and contractions correctly	Teacher Questions • Are students writing and speaking using correct verbs? • Are students using double negatives? • When should students use NON as opposed to NOT? • Are students using correct pronouns? Student Sentence Stems **Using Correct Verb Tenses** • The ___ is ___. • These ___ are ____. • I predict the ___ will... • I concluded that... • The answer is/isn't... • I do/don't agree with...because... • My prediction was not correct because...	• Contextualized Grammar Instruction • Daily Oral Language • Oral Scaffolding • Peer Editing • Reciprocal Teaching • Sentence Mark Up • Sentence Sort

Sentence Stems and Activities Aligned to Cross-Curricular Student Expectations
(subsection c)

Writing		
5(E) continued	**Using Possessive Case/Contractions Correctly** • The graph's ___ shows... • The experiment's ___ is... • My partner's ideas were... • The table's ___ has... • The diagram doesn't show... • The answer can't be ___ because... • The ___ isn't ___. • ___ isn't a characteristic of... • ___ isn't the best representation... • ___ isn't reasonable because... **Using Negatives** • ___ is a non-example. • ___ is a non-example because... • ___ is NOT an example of... • A counter example is... • The solution is not... • The best explanation is not..	
	Examples	
	PK-5 • The **flower's** color is blue. • The boiling point of water **isn't** 25ºC. • A frog is a **non-example** of a plant. 6-8 • The **compound's** density is 1.0 g/ml. • The best conclusion **isn't** that the moon emits light. 9-12 • The **periodic table's** columns are known as families and its rows are called periods. • The **wave's** amplitude **doesn't** exceed its wavelength.	

5(F) write using a variety of grade-appropriate sentence lengths, patterns, and connecting words to combine phrases, clauses, and sentences in increasingly accurate ways as more English is acquired	**Write using a variety of Structures**
	
	Teacher Questions
	• In writing, explain...
	  ○ What are the attributes of...?
	  ○ How would you order ___ from ___ to ___?
	  ○ What will happen if...?
	  ○ What are the similarities between ___ and ___?
	  ○ Predict what the next ___ will be.
	  ○ What can you infer from the ___?
	  ○ What can you conclude from ___?
	
	Student Sentence Stems
	Description
	• A ___ has ___.
	• A ___ has ___, ___, and ___.
	• A ___ is ___, ___, and ___.
	• Additionally ___ has ...
	• ___ is an example of...
	• ___ is an example of.... because ...
		• Dialogue Journal
		• Double Entry Journals
		• Draw & Write
		• Field Notes
		• Free Write
		• Genre Analysis /Imitation
		• Hand Motions for Connecting Words
		• Letters/Editorials
		• Learning Logs and Journals
		• Perspective-Based Writing
		• Read, Write, Pair, Share
		• Summarization Frames

Sentence Stems and Activities Aligned to Cross-Curricular Student Expectations
(subsection c)

Writing

5(F) continued	*Sequence*	
	- First,___. Second,___.	
	- First, ___ and then...	
	- If I put the pictures in order, _____ will be first.	
	Cause and Effect	
	- The ___ is ___, because...	
	- ___ because ___.	
	- The cause is ___. The effect is ___.	
	- ___ was caused by ___.	
	- If ___, then ___.	
	- When ___, then...	
	- The independent variable is ___, and the dependent variable is___.	
	Comparison	
	- A ___ has ___.	
	- A ___ has ___ but a ___ has ___.	
	- ___ and ___ both have...	
	- ___ is the same as ___.	
	- ___ differs from ___ in that...	
	- Although ___ has ___, ___ has ___.	
	- ___on the other hand has...	
	Predictions	
	- The ___ will have...	
	- The ___ will be...	
	- I predict ___ will...	
	- I predict ___ will ___ because...	
	- The next phase will be...	
	- Due to ___, I think ___ will happen.	
	- Consequently, I think...	
	Inferences	
	- I can infer that...	
	- I know ___ because...	
	- My conjecture is...	
	- From the ___, I can infer...	
	Conclusion	
	- All ___ are ___.	
	- ___ are ___.	
	- I concluded...	
	- I can conclude that...	
	- If ___, then ___. Therefore...	

Examples

PK-5

Description
- **Magnets** are **metals**. **Magnets** can pick up paperclips.
- **Magnets** are **metals** and can pick up paperclips.

Sequence
- First, **you add soil**. Second, **you add water**.
- First, **you add soil** and then **add water**.

Sentence Stems and Activities Aligned to
Cross-Curricular Student Expectations
(subsection c)

Writing		
5(F) continued	Examples	
	6-8 **Cause and Effect** • The <u>pattern</u> is <u>getting bigger</u>. • The <u>pattern</u> is <u>getting bigger</u> because <u>you add three color tiles each time</u>. **Comparison** • <u>Photosynthesis</u> happens in the <u>chloroplast</u>. <u>Respiration</u> happens in the <u>mitochondria</u>. • <u>Photosynthesis</u> happens in the <u>chloroplast</u> while <u>respiration</u> happens in the <u>mitochondria</u>. **Prediction** • The <u>speed</u> will <u>increase</u>. • I predict <u>the speed will increase</u> because <u>the ramp is higher</u>. 9-12 **Inferences** • I know it will have a stronger/longer reaction. • I know this <u>element will react easily</u> because of its <u>location on the periodic table</u>. **Conclusion** • <u>**The offspring might be brown.**</u> • I concluded that <u>¾ of the offspring will be brown.</u>	
5(G) narrate, describe, and explain with increasing specificity and detail to fulfill content area writing needs as more English is acquired	**Narrate, Describe, and Explain with Increasing Detail** Teacher Questions • How would you describe ...? • In your own words, explain... • Why did ___ happen? • What else can you say about...? • Will you please restate what ___ said? • Explain how you reached that conclusion. Student Sentence Stems • This is a ... • This is a... and it has/is___ and ___. • The ___ is... • The ___ is ___ because... • ___ best represents ___. • ___ best represents ___ because... • ___ is about... • The most important characteristic is... • ___ is the most important property because... • It is important to remember...	• Free Write • Learning Logs and Journals • Dialogue Journal • Field Notes • Double Entry Journals • Draw & Write • Perspective-Based Writing • Unit Study for ELLs
	Examples	
	PK-5 • This is a <u>planet</u>. This is a <u>planet,</u> and <u>it is large</u> and <u>orbits the Sun</u>. 6-8 • A <u>hurricane is harmful</u>. A <u>hurricane is harmful</u> because <u>it floods the swamps with saltwater</u>. 9-12 • The most important characteristic is the <u>number of protons</u>. • The most important characteristic is the <u>number of protons</u> because <u>each element has a unique number of protons</u>.	

Language Proficiency
Level Descriptors

(subsection d)

§74.4. English Language Proficiency Standards
http://www.tea.state.tx.us/rules/tac/chapter074/ch074a.html.

(d) Proficiency level descriptors.

(1) Listening, Kindergarten-Grade 12. ELLs may be at the beginning, intermediate, advanced, or advanced high stage of English language acquisition in listening. The following proficiency level descriptors for listening are sufficient to describe the overall English language proficiency levels of ELLs in this language domain in order to linguistically accommodate their instruction.

(A) Beginning. Beginning ELLs have little or no ability to understand spoken English in academic and social settings. These students:

(i) struggle to understand simple conversations and simple discussions even when the topics are familiar and the speaker uses linguistic supports such as visuals, slower speech and other verbal cues, and gestures;

(ii) struggle to identify and distinguish individual words and phrases during social and instructional interactions that have not been intentionally modified for ELLs; and

(iii) may not seek clarification in English when failing to comprehend the English they hear; frequently remain silent, watching others for cues.

(B) Intermediate. Intermediate ELLs have the ability to understand simple, high-frequency spoken English used in routine academic and social settings. These students:

(i) usually understand simple or routine directions, as well as short, simple conversations and short, simple discussions on familiar topics; when topics are unfamiliar, require extensive linguistic supports and adaptations such as visuals, slower speech and other verbal cues, simplified language, gestures, and preteaching to preview or build topic-related vocabulary;

(ii) often identify and distinguish key words and phrases necessary to understand the general meaning during social and basic instructional interactions that have not been intentionally modified for ELLs; and

(iii) have the ability to seek clarification in English when failing to comprehend the English they hear by requiring/requesting the speaker to repeat, slow down, or rephrase speech.

(C) Advanced. Advanced ELLs have the ability to understand, with second language acquisition support, grade-appropriate spoken English used in academic and social settings. These students:

(i) usually understand longer, more elaborated directions, conversations, and discussions on familiar and some unfamiliar topics, but sometimes need processing time and sometimes depend on visuals, verbal cues, and gestures to support understanding;

(ii) understand most main points, most important details, and some implicit information during social and basic instructional interactions that have not been intentionally modified for ELLs; and

(iii) occasionally require/request the speaker to repeat, slow down, or rephrase to clarify the meaning of the English they hear.

(D) Advanced high. Advanced high ELLs have the ability to understand, with minimal second language acquisition support, grade-appropriate spoken English used in academic and social settings. These students:

(i) understand longer, elaborated directions, conversations, and discussions on familiar and unfamiliar topics with occasional need for processing time and with little dependence on visuals, verbal cues, and gestures; some exceptions when complex academic or highly specialized language is used;

(ii) understand main points, important details, and implicit information at a level nearly comparable to native English-speaking peers during social and instructional interactions; and

(iii) rarely require/request the speaker to repeat, slow down, or rephrase to clarify the meaning of the English they hear.

(2) Speaking, Kindergarten-Grade 12. ELLs may be at the beginning, intermediate, advanced, or advanced high stage of English language acquisition in speaking. The following proficiency level descriptors for speaking are sufficient to describe the overall English language proficiency levels of ELLs in this language domain in order to linguistically accommodate their instruction.

(A) Beginning. Beginning ELLs have little or no ability to speak English in academic and social settings. These students:

(i) mainly speak using single words and short phrases consisting of recently practiced, memorized, or highly familiar material to get immediate needs met; may be hesitant to speak and often give up in their attempts to communicate;

(ii) speak using a very limited bank of high-frequency, high-need, concrete vocabulary, including key words and expressions needed for basic communication in academic and social contexts;

(iii) lack the knowledge of English grammar necessary to connect ideas and speak in sentences; can sometimes produce sentences using recently practiced, memorized, or highly familiar material;

(iv) exhibit second language acquisition errors that may hinder overall communication, particularly when trying to convey information beyond memorized, practiced, or highly familiar material; and

(v) typically use pronunciation that significantly inhibits communication.

(B) Intermediate. Intermediate ELLs have the ability to speak in a simple manner using English commonly heard in routine academic and social settings. These students:

(i) are able to express simple, original messages, speak using sentences, and participate in short conversations and classroom interactions; may hesitate frequently and for long periods to think about how to communicate desired meaning;

(ii) speak simply using basic vocabulary needed in everyday social interactions and routine academic contexts; rarely have vocabulary to speak in detail;

(iii) exhibit an emerging awareness of English grammar and speak using mostly simple sentence structures and simple tenses; are most comfortable speaking in present tense;

(iv) exhibit second language acquisition errors that may hinder overall communication when trying to use complex or less familiar English; and

(v) use pronunciation that can usually be understood by people accustomed to interacting with ELLs.

(C) Advanced. Advanced ELLs have the ability to speak using grade-appropriate English, with second language acquisition support, in academic and social settings. These students:

(i) are able to participate comfortably in most conversations and academic discussions on familiar topics, with some pauses to restate, repeat, or search for words and phrases to clarify meaning;

(ii) discuss familiar academic topics using content-based terms and common abstract vocabulary; can usually speak in some detail on familiar topics;

(iii) have a grasp of basic grammar features, including a basic ability to narrate and describe in present, past, and future tenses; have an emerging ability to use complex sentences and complex grammar features;

(iv) make errors that interfere somewhat with communication when using complex grammar structures, long sentences, and less familiar words and expressions; and

(v) may mispronounce words, but use pronunciation that can usually be understood by people not accustomed to interacting with ELLs.

(D) Advanced high. Advanced high ELLs have the ability to speak using grade-appropriate English, with minimal second language acquisition support, in academic and social settings. These students:

(i) are able to participate in extended discussions on a variety of social and grade-appropriate academic topics with only occasional disruptions, hesitations, or pauses;

(ii) communicate effectively using abstract and content-based vocabulary during classroom instructional tasks, with some exceptions when low-frequency or academically demanding vocabulary is needed; use many of the same idioms and colloquialisms as their native English-speaking peers;

(iii) can use English grammar structures and complex sentences to narrate and describe at a level nearly comparable to native English-speaking peers;

(iv) make few second language acquisition errors that interfere with overall communication; and

(v) may mispronounce words, but rarely use pronunciation that interferes with overall communication.

(3) Reading, Kindergarten-Grade 1. ELLs in Kindergarten and Grade 1 may be at the beginning, intermediate, advanced, or advanced high stage of English language acquisition in reading. The following proficiency level descriptors for reading are sufficient to describe the overall English

language proficiency levels of ELLs in this language domain in order to linguistically accommodate their instruction and should take into account developmental stages of emergent readers.

(A) Beginning. Beginning ELLs have little or no ability to use the English language to build foundational reading skills. These students:

(i) derive little or no meaning from grade-appropriate stories read aloud in English, unless the stories are:

(I) read in short "chunks;"

(II) controlled to include the little English they know such as language that is high frequency, concrete, and recently practiced; and

(III) accompanied by ample visual supports such as illustrations, gestures, pantomime, and objects and by linguistic supports such as careful enunciation and slower speech;

(ii) begin to recognize and understand environmental print in English such as signs, labeled items, names of peers, and logos; and

(iii) have difficulty decoding most grade-appropriate English text because they:

(I) understand the meaning of very few words in English; and

(II) struggle significantly with sounds in spoken English words and with sound-symbol relationships due to differences between their primary language and English.

(B) Intermediate. Intermediate ELLs have a limited ability to use the English language to build foundational reading skills. These students:

(i) demonstrate limited comprehension (key words and general meaning) of grade-appropriate stories read aloud in English, unless the stories include:

(I) predictable story lines;

(II) highly familiar topics;

(III) primarily high-frequency, concrete vocabulary;

(IV) short, simple sentences; and

(V) visual and linguistic supports;

(ii) regularly recognize and understand common environmental print in English such as signs, labeled items, names of peers, logos; and

(iii) have difficulty decoding grade-appropriate English text because they:

(I) understand the meaning of only those English words they hear frequently; and

(II) struggle with some sounds in English words and some sound-symbol relationships due to differences between their primary language and English.

(C) Advanced. Advanced ELLs have the ability to use the English language, with second language acquisition support, to build foundational reading skills. These students:

(i) demonstrate comprehension of most main points and most supporting ideas in grade-appropriate stories read aloud in English, although they may still depend on visual and linguistic supports to gain or confirm meaning;

(ii) recognize some basic English vocabulary and high-frequency words in isolated print; and

(iii) with second language acquisition support, are able to decode most grade-appropriate English text because they:

(I) understand the meaning of most grade-appropriate English words; and

(II) have little difficulty with English sounds and sound-symbol relationships that result from differences between their primary language and English.

(D) Advanced high. Advanced high ELLs have the ability to use the English language, with minimal second language acquisition support, to build foundational reading skills. These students:

(i) demonstrate, with minimal second language acquisition support and at a level nearly comparable to native English-speaking peers, comprehension of main points and supporting ideas (explicit and implicit) in grade-appropriate stories read aloud in English;

(ii) with some exceptions, recognize sight vocabulary and high-frequency words to a degree nearly comparable to that of native English-speaking peers; and

(iii) with minimal second language acquisition support, have an ability to decode and understand grade-appropriate English text at a level nearly comparable to native English-speaking peers.

(4) Reading, Grades 2-12. ELLs in Grades 2-12 may be at the beginning, intermediate, advanced, or advanced high stage of English language acquisition in reading. The following proficiency level descriptors for reading are sufficient to describe the overall English language proficiency levels of ELLs in this language domain in order to linguistically accommodate their instruction.

(A) Beginning. Beginning ELLs have little or no ability to read and understand English used in academic and social contexts. These students:

(i) read and understand the very limited recently practiced, memorized, or highly familiar English they have learned; vocabulary predominantly includes:

(I) environmental print;

(II) some very high-frequency words; and

(III) concrete words that can be represented by pictures;

(ii) read slowly, word by word;

(iii) have a very limited sense of English language structures;

(iv) comprehend predominantly isolated familiar words and phrases; comprehend some sentences in highly routine contexts or recently practiced, highly familiar text;

(v) are highly dependent on visuals and prior knowledge to derive meaning from text in English; and

(vi) are able to apply reading comprehension skills in English only when reading texts written for this level.

(B) Intermediate. Intermediate ELLs have the ability to read and understand simple, high-frequency English used in routine academic and social contexts. These students:

(i) read and understand English vocabulary on a somewhat wider range of topics and with increased depth; vocabulary predominantly includes:

(I) everyday oral language;

(II) literal meanings of common words;

(III) routine academic language and terms; and

(IV) commonly used abstract language such as terms used to describe basic feelings;

(ii) often read slowly and in short phrases; may re-read to clarify meaning;

(iii) have a growing understanding of basic, routinely used English language structures;

(iv) understand simple sentences in short, connected texts, but are dependent on visual cues, topic familiarity, prior knowledge, pretaught topic-related vocabulary, story predictability, and teacher/peer assistance to sustain comprehension;

(v) struggle to independently read and understand grade-level texts; and

(vi) are able to apply basic and some higher-order comprehension skills when reading texts that are linguistically accommodated and/or simplified for this level.

(C) Advanced. Advanced ELLs have the ability to read and understand, with second language acquisition support, grade-appropriate English used in academic and social contexts. These students:

(i) read and understand, with second language acquisition support, a variety of grade-appropriate English vocabulary used in social and academic contexts:

(I) with second language acquisition support, read and understand grade-appropriate concrete and abstract vocabulary, but have difficulty with less commonly encountered words;

(II) demonstrate an emerging ability to understand words and phrases beyond their literal meaning; and

(III) understand multiple meanings of commonly used words;

(ii) read longer phrases and simple sentences from familiar text with appropriate rate and speed;

(iii) are developing skill in using their growing familiarity with English language structures to construct meaning of grade-appropriate text; and

(iv) are able to apply basic and higher-order comprehension skills when reading grade-appropriate text, but are still occasionally dependent on visuals, teacher/peer assistance, and other linguistically accommodated text features to determine or clarify meaning, particularly with unfamiliar topics.

(D) Advanced high. Advanced high ELLs have the ability to read and understand, with minimal second language acquisition support, grade-appropriate English used in academic and social contexts. These students:

(i) read and understand vocabulary at a level nearly comparable to that of their native English-speaking peers, with some exceptions when low-frequency or specialized vocabulary is used;

(ii) generally read grade-appropriate, familiar text with appropriate rate, speed, intonation, and expression;

(iii) are able to, at a level nearly comparable to native English-speaking peers, use their familiarity with English language structures to construct meaning of grade-appropriate text; and

(iv) are able to apply, with minimal second language acquisition support and at a level nearly comparable to native English-speaking peers, basic and higher-order comprehension skills when reading grade-appropriate text.

(5) Writing, Kindergarten-Grade 1. ELLs in Kindergarten and Grade 1 may be at the beginning, intermediate, advanced, or advanced high stage of English language acquisition in writing. The following proficiency level descriptors for writing are sufficient to describe the overall English language proficiency levels of ELLs in this language domain in order to linguistically accommodate their instruction and should take into account developmental stages of emergent writers.

(A) Beginning. Beginning ELLs have little or no ability to use the English language to build foundational writing skills. These students:

(i) are unable to use English to explain self-generated writing such as stories they have created or other personal expressions, including emergent forms of writing (pictures, letter-like forms, mock words, scribbling, etc.);

(ii) know too little English to participate meaningfully in grade-appropriate shared writing activities using the English language;

(iii) cannot express themselves meaningfully in self-generated, connected written text in English beyond the level of high-frequency, concrete words, phrases, or short sentences that have been recently practiced and/or memorized; and

(iv) may demonstrate little or no awareness of English print conventions.

(B) Intermediate. Intermediate ELLs have a limited ability to use the English language to build foundational writing skills. These students:

(i) know enough English to explain briefly and simply self-generated writing, including emergent forms of writing, as long as the topic is highly familiar and concrete and requires very high-frequency English;

(ii) can participate meaningfully in grade-appropriate shared writing activities using the English language only when the writing topic is highly familiar and concrete and requires very high-frequency English;

(iii) express themselves meaningfully in self-generated, connected written text in English when their writing is limited to short sentences featuring simple, concrete English used frequently in class; and

(iv) frequently exhibit features of their primary language when writing in English such as primary language words, spelling patterns, word order, and literal translating.

(C) Advanced. Advanced ELLs have the ability to use the English language to build, with second language acquisition support, foundational writing skills. These students:

(i) use predominantly grade-appropriate English to explain, in some detail, most self-generated writing, including emergent forms of writing;

(ii) can participate meaningfully, with second language acquisition support, in most grade-appropriate shared writing activities using the English language;

(iii) although second language acquisition support is needed, have an emerging ability to express themselves in self-generated, connected written text in English in a grade-appropriate manner; and

(iv) occasionally exhibit second language acquisition errors when writing in English.

(D) Advanced high. Advanced high ELLs have the ability to use the English language to build, with minimal second language acquisition support, foundational writing skills. These students:

(i) use English at a level of complexity and detail nearly comparable to that of native English-speaking peers when explaining self-generated writing, including emergent forms of writing;

(ii) can participate meaningfully in most grade-appropriate shared writing activities using the English language; and

(iii) although minimal second language acquisition support may be needed, express themselves in self-generated, connected written text in English in a manner nearly comparable to their native English-speaking peers.

(6) Writing, Grades 2-12. ELLs in Grades 2-12 may be at the beginning, intermediate, advanced, or advanced high stage of English language acquisition in writing. The following proficiency level descriptors for writing are sufficient to describe the overall English language proficiency levels of ELLs in this language domain in order to linguistically accommodate their instruction.

(A) Beginning. Beginning ELLs lack the English vocabulary and grasp of English language structures necessary to address grade-appropriate writing tasks meaningfully. These students:

> (i) have little or no ability to use the English language to express ideas in writing and engage meaningfully in grade-appropriate writing assignments in content area instruction;

> (ii) lack the English necessary to develop or demonstrate elements of grade-appropriate writing such as focus and coherence, conventions, organization, voice, and development of ideas in English; and

> (iii) exhibit writing features typical at this level, including:

>> (I) ability to label, list, and copy;

>> (II) high-frequency words/phrases and short, simple sentences (or even short paragraphs) based primarily on recently practiced, memorized, or highly familiar material; this type of writing may be quite accurate;

>> (III) present tense used primarily; and

>> (IV) frequent primary language features (spelling patterns, word order, literal translations, and words from the student's primary language) and other errors associated with second language acquisition may significantly hinder or prevent understanding, even for individuals accustomed to the writing of ELLs.

(B) Intermediate. Intermediate ELLs have enough English vocabulary and enough grasp of English language structures to address grade-appropriate writing tasks in a limited way. These students:

> (i) have a limited ability to use the English language to express ideas in writing and engage meaningfully in grade-appropriate writing assignments in content area instruction;

> (ii) are limited in their ability to develop or demonstrate elements of grade-appropriate writing in English; communicate best when topics are highly familiar and concrete, and require simple, high-frequency English; and

> (iii) exhibit writing features typical at this level, including:

>> (I) simple, original messages consisting of short, simple sentences; frequent inaccuracies occur when creating or taking risks beyond familiar English;

>> (II) high-frequency vocabulary; academic writing often has an oral tone;

>> (III) loosely connected text with limited use of cohesive devices or repetitive use, which may cause gaps in meaning;

>> (IV) repetition of ideas due to lack of vocabulary and language structures;

>> (V) present tense used most accurately; simple future and past tenses, if attempted, are used inconsistently or with frequent inaccuracies;

(VI) undetailed descriptions, explanations, and narrations; difficulty expressing abstract ideas;

(VII) primary language features and errors associated with second language acquisition may be frequent; and

(VIII) some writing may be understood only by individuals accustomed to the writing of ELLs; parts of the writing may be hard to understand even for individuals accustomed to ELL writing.

(C) Advanced. Advanced ELLs have enough English vocabulary and command of English language structures to address grade-appropriate writing tasks, although second language acquisition support is needed. These students:

(i) are able to use the English language, with second language acquisition support, to express ideas in writing and engage meaningfully in grade-appropriate writing assignments in content-area instruction;

(ii) know enough English to be able to develop or demonstrate elements of grade-appropriate writing in English, although second language acquisition support is particularly needed when topics are abstract, academically challenging, or unfamiliar; and

(iii) exhibit writing features typical at this level, including:

(I) grasp of basic verbs, tenses, grammar features, and sentence patterns; partial grasp of more complex verbs, tenses, grammar features, and sentence patterns;

(II) emerging grade-appropriate vocabulary; academic writing has a more academic tone;

(III) use of a variety of common cohesive devices, although some redundancy may occur;

(IV) narrations, explanations, and descriptions developed in some detail with emerging clarity; quality or quantity declines when abstract ideas are expressed, academic demands are high, or low-frequency vocabulary is required;

(V) occasional second language acquisition errors; and

(VI) communications are usually understood by individuals not accustomed to the writing of ELLs.

(D) Advanced high. Advanced high ELLs have acquired the English vocabulary and command of English language structures necessary to address grade-appropriate writing tasks with minimal second language acquisition support. These students:

(i) are able to use the English language, with minimal second language acquisition support, to express ideas in writing and engage meaningfully in grade-appropriate writing assignments in content area instruction;

(ii) know enough English to be able to develop or demonstrate, with minimal second language acquisition support, elements of grade-appropriate writing in English; and

(iii) exhibit writing features typical at this level, including:

(I) nearly comparable to writing of native English-speaking peers in clarity and precision with regard to English vocabulary and language structures, with occasional exceptions when writing about academically complex ideas, abstract ideas, or topics requiring low-frequency vocabulary;

(II) occasional difficulty with naturalness of phrasing and expression; and

(III) errors associated with second language acquisition are minor and usually limited to low-frequency words and structures; errors rarely interfere with communication.

(e) Effective date. The provisions of this section supersede the ESL standards specified in Chapter 128 of this title (relating to Texas Essential Knowledge and Skills for Spanish Language Arts and English as a Second Language) upon the effective date of this section.

Source: http://www.tea.state.tx.us/rules/tac/chapter074/ch074a.html

ELPS Linguistic Accommodation by Proficiency Level Self-Assessment

Rate the current level of awareness of the English Language Proficiency Standards at your district or campus.

A: Always
M: Mostly

S: Sometimes
N: Never

Indicator	A	M	S	N	Comments/Questions
I am aware of the level of language proficiency of the English Language Learners I teach.					
I am aware of specific instructional strategies to support ELLs at various levels of English language proficiency.					
I am aware of specific English language district and classroom resources that enhance comprehension for ELLs at various levels of proficiency.					
I am aware of specific native language district and classroom resources that enhance comprehension for ELLs at various levels of proficiency.					
I differentiate instruction to meet students' needs at various levels of language proficiency.					
I provide a variety of resources for English Language Learners at various levels of proficiency.					

Summaries of ELPS Proficiency Level Descriptors*

Please refer to actual proficiency level descriptors to plan instruction.

Level	Listening (d1: k-12) The student comprehends...	Speaking (d2: k-12) The student speaks...	Reading (d4: 2-12) The student reads...	Writing (d6: 2-12) The student writes...
Beginning (A)	1A(i) few simple conversations with linguistic support 1A(ii) **modified conversation** 1A(iii) few words, **does not seek clarification**, watches others for cues	2A(i) using **single words and short phrases** with practiced material; tends to give up on attempts 2A(ii) using **limited bank of key vocabulary** 2A(iii) with **recently practiced familiar material** 2A(iv) with **frequent errors that hinder** communication 2A(v) with **pronunciation that inhibits communication**	4A(i) little except recently practiced terms, **environmental print**, high frequency words, **concrete words represented by pictures** 4A(ii) **slowly, word by word** 4A(iii) with very limited sense of English structure 4A(iv) with comprehension of **practiced, familiar text** 4A(v) with need for **visuals and prior knowledge** 4A(vi) modified and adapted text	6A(i) with **little ability to use English** 6A(ii) **without focus** and coherence, conventions, organization, voice 6A(iii) labels, lists, and copies of printed text and **high-frequency words/phrases,** short and simple, practiced sentences primarily in **present tense with frequent errors** that hinder or prevent understanding
Intermediate (B)	1B(i) unfamiliar language with linguistic supports and adaptations 1B(ii) unmodified conversation with **key words and phrases** 1B(iii) with **requests for clarification** by asking speaker to repeat, slow down, or rephrase speech	2B(i) **with simple messages** and hesitation to think about meaning 2B(ii) using **basic vocabulary** 2B(iii) with **simple sentence structures** and present tense 2B(iv) with errors that inhibit unfamiliar communication 2B(v) with **pronunciation** generally **understood** by those familiar with English Language Learners	4B(i) **wider range of topics:** and everyday academic language 4B(ii) **slowly and rereads** 4B(iii) basic language structures 4B(iv) simple sentences **with visual cues, pretaught vocabulary and interaction** 4B(v) **grade-level texts** with difficulty 4B(vi) at high level with **linguistic accommodation**	6B(i) with **limited ability to use English** in content area writing 6B(ii) best on **topics that are highly familiar** with simple English 6B(iii) with **simple oral tone in messages,** high-frequency vocabulary, loosely connected text, repetition of ideas, **mostly in the present tense,** undetailed descriptions, and **frequent errors**
Advanced (C)	1C(i) with some processing time, **visuals, verbal cues, and gestures; for unfamiliar conversations** 1C(ii) most unmodified interaction 1C(iii) with occasional **requests** for the speaker to slow down, repeat, rephrase, and **clarify meaning**	2C(i) in conversations with some **pauses to restate, repeat, and clarify** 2C(ii) using **content-based and abstract** terms on familiar topics 2C(iii) with **past, present, and future tenses** 2C(iv) using **complex sentences** and grammar with some errors 2C(v) with **pronunciation usually understood by most**	4C(i) **abstract** grade appropriate text 4C(ii) **longer phrases and familiar sentences** appropriately 4C(iii) while developing the ability to construct meaning from text 4C(iv) at **high comprehension level** with linguistic support for unfamiliar topics and to clarify meaning	6C(i) grade appropriate **ideas with second language support** 6C(ii) with extra need for second language **support when topics are technical and abstract** 6C(iii) with a grasp of basic English usage and some understanding of complex usage with **emerging grade-appropriate vocabulary** and a more academic tone
Advanced High (D)	1D(i) longer discussions on **unfamiliar topics** 1D(ii) spoken information nearly **comparable to native speaker** 1D(iii) with **few requests** for speaker to slow down, repeat, or rephrase	2D(i) in **extended discussions** with few pauses 2D(ii) using **abstract content-based vocabulary** except low frequency terms; using idioms 2D(iii) with grammar **nearly comparable to native speaker** 2D(iv) with **few errors** blocking communication 2D(v) **occasional mispronunciation**	4D(i) **nearly comparable to native speakers** 4D(ii) **grade appropriate familiar text** appropriately 4D(iii) while constructing meaning at near native ability level 4D(iv) with **high level comprehension with minimal linguistic support**	6D(i) grade appropriate **content area ideas with little need for linguistic support** 6D(ii) develop and demonstrate **grade appropriate writing** 6D (iii) **nearly comparable to native** speakers with clarity and precision, with **occasional difficulties** with naturalness of language.

*These summaries are not appropriate to use in formally identifying student proficiency levels for TELPAS. TELPAS assessment and training materials are provided by the Texas Education Agency Student Assessment Division: http://www.tea.state.tx.us/index3.aspx?id=3300&menu_id3=793

Linguistic Accommodations for each Proficiency Level*

Sequence of Language Development	Communicating and Scaffolding Instruction			
	Listening	Speaking	Reading	Writing
Beginning Students (A)	Teachers... • Allow use of **same language peer and native language support** • Expect student to struggle to understand simple conversations • Use **gestures and movement** and other linguistic support to communicate language and expectations	Teachers... • Provide short sentence stems and single words for practice before conversations • **Allow some nonparticipation** in simple conversations • Provide **word bank** of key vocabulary • **Model pronunciation of social and academic language**	Teachers... • Organize reading in **chunks** • Practice **high frequency, concrete terms** • Use **visual and linguistic supports** • Explain classroom **environmental print** • Use adapted text	Teachers... • **Allow drawing and use of native language** to express concepts • Allow student to use high frequency recently memorized; and **short, simple, sentences** • Provide **short, simple sentence stems** with present tense and high frequency vocabulary
Intermediate (B)	• Provide **visuals, slower speech, verbal cues, simplified language** • **Preteach vocabulary** before discussions and lectures • **Teach phrases** for student to request speakers to repeat, slow down, or rephrase speech	• Allow extra **processing time** • Provide **sentence stems** with simple sentence structures and tenses • Model and provide practice in **pronunciation of academic terms**	• Allow wide range of reading • Allow grade-level comprehension and analysis of tasks including **drawing and** use of **native language** and peer collaboration • Provide high level of **visual and linguistic supports** with adapted text and **pretaught vocabulary**	• Allow **drawing and use of native language** to express academic concepts • Allow writing on **familiar, concrete topics** • **Avoid assessment of language errors** in content area writing • Provide **simple sentence stems and scaffolded writing assignments**
Advanced (C)	• Allow some **processing time, visuals, verbal cues, and gestures** for unfamiliar conversations • Provide opportunities for student to **request clarification**, repetition and rephrasing	• **Allow extra time after pauses** • Provide **sentence stems** with past, present, future tenses and **complex grammar,** and vocabulary with **content-based and abstract terms**	• Allow abstract grade-level reading comprehension and analysis with **peer support** • Provide **visual and linguistic supports** including **adapted text** for unfamiliar topics	• Provide **grade-level appropriate writing tasks** • Allow abstract and technical writing with linguistic support including teacher **modeling and student interaction** • Provide complex **sentence stems** for **scaffolded writing assignments**
Advanced High (D)	• Allow some extra time when academic material is complex and unfamiliar • Provide **visuals, verbal cues, and gestures** when material is complex and unfamiliar	• Opportunities for **extended discussions** • Provide **sentence stems with past,** present, future tenses and **complex grammar** and vocabulary with **content-based and abstract terms**	• Allow abstract grade-level reading • Provide minimal **visual and linguistic supports** • Allow grade level comprehension and analysis tasks with **peer collaboration**	• Provide complex **grade-level appropriate writing tasks** • Allow abstract and technical writing with **minimal linguistic support** • Use **genre analysis** to identify and use features of advanced English writing

Guidelines at specific proficiency levels may be beneficial for students at all levels of proficiency depending on the context of instructional delivery, materials, and students' background knowledge.

Differentiating by Language Level
Instructional Planning Guide

Advanced/Advanced High	Intermediate	Beginners
<ul><li>Visuals for academic vocabulary and concepts</li><li>Grade-level text</li><li>Complex sentence stems</li><li>Preteaching low-frequency academic vocabulary</li><li>Peer interaction</li><li>Verbal scaffolding as needed</li><li>Grade level writing tasks</li><li>Gestures for memorization of academic concepts</li><li>Modeling</li><li>Graphic organizers</li><li>Manipulatives</li></ul>	<ul><li>Visuals for academic vocabulary and concepts</li><li>Adapted grade level text</li><li>Sentence stems</li><li>Preteaching academic vocabulary</li><li>Peer interaction</li><li>Verbal scaffolding</li><li>Adapted writing tasks with scaffolding</li><li>Gestures for memorization of academic concepts</li><li>Modeling</li><li>Graphic organizers</li><li>Manipulatives</li></ul>	<ul><li>Visuals for classroom vocabulary and academic concepts</li><li>Native language and adapted grade level text</li><li>Short, simple sentence stems</li><li>Preteaching social and academic vocabulary</li><li>Peer interaction (same language peer as needed)</li><li>Extensive verbal scaffolding</li><li>Adapted writing tasks with drawing and scaffolding</li><li>Gestures (basic and academic concepts)</li><li>Modeling</li><li>Graphic organizers</li><li>Manipulatives</li><li>Preteaching functional language (stems for social interaction)</li><li>Pronunciation of social/academic language</li><li>Slower, simplified speech</li><li>Instruction in high frequency concrete social vocabulary</li><li>Use of native language for key concepts</li><li>Verbal cues</li><li>Chunking use of information in print</li><li>Word bank</li></ul>

Differentiating by Language Level
Instructional Planning Template

Grade Level/Topic:	Content Objective:
Key Vocabulary & Concepts:	Language Objective:

Tasks and Accommodations for Advanced/Advanced High	Accommodation to Support Intermediate Students	Accommodations to Support Beginners

This page is intentionally left blank.

Guide to Terms and Activities

Accountable Conversation Questions:

Place the following poster in your room:

> **What to say instead of "I Don't Know"**
>
> - May I please have some more information?
> - May I have some time to think?
> - Would you please repeat the question?
> - Where could I find information about that?
>
> *Please speak in complete sentences.*

Model the way students can use the poster questions when they are unsure about what to say when called on by the teacher. (Seidlitz & Perryman, 2008). Explain that when they are called on for a response, they can either respond, or ask for help and then respond. Newcomer English Language Learners should not be pressured to speak in front of the class if they have not yet begun to show early production levels of speech proficiency. Students should be encouraged, but not forced to speak when in the silent period of language development (Krashen, 1982).

Academic language: Specialized vocabulary and structures tend to be more abstract, complex, and challenging and are found with high frequency in classroom oral and written discourse.

Adapted Text: Adaptations in text helps struggling students comprehend academic language. Some methods include: graphic organizers, outlines, highlighted text, taped text, margin notes, native language texts, native language glossaries, and word lists (Echevarria, Vogt & Short, 2008)

Advance Organizers: Information given to students prior to reading or instruction help them organize information they encounter during instruction (Mayer, 2003). Advance organizers should involve both activating prior knowledge and organizing new information. Examples include: graphic organizers, anticipation guides, KWL, guided notes, etc.

Anticipation Chat: Prior to instruction, a teacher facilitates a conversation between students about the content to be learned. The teacher opens the discussion by having the students make inferences about what they are going to learn based on prior knowledge, experiences and limited information about the new concepts (Zwiers, 2008).

Anticipation Guides: This is a structured series of statements given to students before instruction. Students choose to agree or disagree with the statements either individually or in groups. After instruction, students revisit the statements and discuss whether have changed their minds about the statements, based on what they have learned. (Head, M. H. & Readence, J. 1986).

Backwards Book Walk: Students scan a non-fiction text, briefly looking at headings, illustrations, captions, key words, and other text features before reading a book. After the scan, students discuss what they believe they will learn from the text. (Echevarria & Vogt, 2008)

Book Reviews: After being immersed in the book review genre, English Language Learners write short reviews which can then be published for others to read. (Samway, K., 2006)

Brick words: Brick words are content specific vocabulary. (Dutro, S., & Moran, C., 2003).

Brick and Mortar Cards: Students are given five "brick" cards with academic vocabulary (content area terms) and are instructed to organize them in a way they think makes sense. Afterward, they have to link the cards together using the language. They write the language they are using on "mortar" cards that tie the concepts together. Students may need lists of sentence terms and connecting words to facilitate the process. (Zwiers, 2008)

CALLA Approach: This is an approach to teaching English Language Learners that involves the explicit teaching of language learning strategies, academic content, and language skills with scaffolding, active engaged learning, and language use. (Chamot, A. & O'Malley, J., 1994)

CCAP (Communicative Cognitive Approach to Pronunciation): This is a five-step process for assisting English Language Learners in improving pronunciation. (Celce-Murcia, M., Brinton, D. & Goodwin. J, 1996 as cited in Flores M., 1998)

- Description and analysis of the pronunciation feature
- Listening/Discrimination activities (see segmental/supra segmental practice below).
- Controlled practice and feedback
- Guided practice and feedback
- Communicative practice

Canned Questions: Students are given a series of question stems ranging from the lowest to the highest level of Bloom's Taxonomy so that they can participate in discussions about a topic. For example:

- "What is..."
- "How do..."
- What would be a better approach to..."
- "How do you know that..." (Echevarria & Vogt, 2008)

Choose the Words: During this activity, students select words from a word wall or word list to use in a conversation or in writing.

Chunking Input: Chunking means to break up material into smaller units for easier comprehension. Visual and auditory information can be chunked so that students have time to discuss new information, pay attention to details, and create schema for organizing new information.

Cloze Sentences: Fill in the blank sentences help students process academic text. (Taylor, 1953; Gibbons, 2002)

Compare, Contrast, Analogy & Metaphor Frames: These sentence frames help students organize schema for new words (Marzano, 2001 & Hill, J. & Flynn, K. 2006)

For example:

- Compare: ___ is similar to ___ in that both....
- Contrast: ___ is different from ___ in that ...
- Analogy: ___ is to ___ as ___ is to ____
- Metaphor: I think ___ is like/is... because...

Comprehension Strategies: Strategies help proficient readers understand what they read. These strategies are used in different kinds of text, can be taught, and when they are taught, students are likely to use them. Strategies include: prediction, self-questioning, monitoring, determining importance, and summarizing. (Echevarria, Vogt, & Short, 2008; Dole, Duffy, Roehler, & Pearson, 1991; Baker, 2004)

Concept Attainment: This Jerome Bruner strategy instructs teachers to provide examples and non-examples of concepts to students. Then teachers can ask students to categorize the examples. Over time, students develop conceptual categories at increasing levels of depth and understanding. (Boulware, B.J., & Crow, M., 2008; Bruner, J., 1967)

Concept Definition Map: This visual organizer enables students to process a term. (Echevarria, Vogt, & Short, 2008.) Four questions are asked:

- What is the term?
- What is it?
- What is it like?
- What are some examples?

Concept Mapping: This is a technique for making a visual diagram of the relationship between concepts. Concept maps begin with a single concept written in a square or circle. New concepts are listed and connected with lines and shapes creating a web that shows the relationship between the ideas. (Novak, J.D., 1995)

Content Specific Stems: In this activity, incomplete sentences are directly tied to content concepts to scaffold the development of language structures that provide the opportunity for conversation and writing.

Conga Line: During this activity, students form two lines facing one another. Students in each row share ideas, review concepts, or ask one another questions. After the first discussion, one row moves and the other remains stationary so that each student now has a new partner. (Echevarria & Vogt, 2008)

Content-Specific Stems: In this activity, sentence stems using content specific vocabulary are provided to students. For example, instead of a general stem such as, "In my opinion..." a content specific stem would be, "In my opinion the Declaration of Independence is significant because..."

Contextualized Grammar Instruction: Teaching grammar in mini-lessons demonstrates specific, meaningful tasks that students will perform. The purpose of the grammar instruction is to enable students to communicate verbally or to write more effectively. (Weaver, 1996)

Cornell Notes: Students use this method of note-taking in which a paper is divided into two columns. In one large column students take traditional notes in modified outline form. In the other column, students write key vocabulary terms and questions. (Paulk, Walter, 2000).

Creating Analogies: This method is used to generate comparisons using the frame: ____ is to

____ as ___ is to ____. (Marzano, R., Pickering, D., & Pollock, J, 2001)

Daily Oral Language: This strategy for teaching English usage involves five minute mini-lessons where students view a list of sentences with incorrect English usage. Students learn correct usage by correcting the mistakes in the sentences. (Vail, N. & Papenfuss, J., 1993).

Dialogue Journal: A dialogue journal is exchanged between the student and teacher or between two or more students. The journal focuses on academic topics, and the language used by the teacher and student should be content focused and academic. (Samway, K., 2006)

Direct Teaching of Affixes: Lessons on prefixes and suffixes build knowledge of English word structure. (White, Sowell, & Yanagihara, 1989)

Direct Teaching of Cognates: Lessons on words that sound the same in the primary language and the target language help students learn quickly. For a list of Spanish and English cognates see: http://www.colorincolorado.org/pdfs/articles/cognates.pdf . Students must be careful of false cognates, words that sound the same in the primary and target language, but do not have the same meaning. For a list of false Spanish/English cognates see: http://www.platiquemos-letstalk.com/Extras/Articles/FalseCognates/FalseCongnatesMain.htm

Direct Teaching of Word Roots: In this activity, students learn Greek and Latin roots that form the base of many words in English. A partial list of roots can be found here: https://www.msu.edu/~defores1/gre/roots/gre_rts_afx2.htm

Directionality Sort: In groups, students are given copies of texts in various languages. Each group must sort the texts based on perceived directionality. Is the text written from top to bottom then left to right? Is the text written right to left, then top to bottom? For newspapers showing letters and characters used in a variety of languages see: www.newoxxo.com

Discovery Learning: This is an inquiry-based approach to instruction in which teachers create problems and dilemmas through which students construct knowledge and representations of knowledge. Ideas, hypotheses, and explanations continue to be revised as learning takes place. (Bruner, J.S. 1967). This discovery approach has been criticized by some (Marzano, 2001; Kirschner, P. A., Sweller, J. & Clark, R. E. (2006) for teaching skills to novices who don't have adequate background and language to be able to learn new content. Teachers of English Language Learners must be careful to preteach content area functional language and set goals and objectives for the lesson when teaching English Language Learners using a discovery approach.

Discussion Starter Cards: Small cards containing sentence starters are given to students to use when beginning an academic conversation or when seeking ways to extend a conversation. For example: In my opinion..., I think..., Another possibility is ... etc. (Thornberry, 2005)

Double Entry Journals: This is a two-column journal used for reflective writing about texts. In one column, students write words, phrases, or ideas they found interesting or significant while reading. In the other column, students write the reasons they found the words significant, or they list ways they could use them in their own writing. (Samway, K, 2006)

Draw & Write: This exercise allows English Language Learners to express their knowledge of academic content while drawing and writing. Students may use their native language to express ideas but are encouraged to express new concepts using English. (Adapted from: Samway, K., 2006)

DRTA (Directed Reading-Thinking Activity): In this activity, the teacher stops regularly during reading to have students make and justify predictions. Questions might be: What do you think is going to happen? Why do you think that will happen next? Is there another possibility? What made you think that? (Echevarria, Vogt, & Short, 2008)

Experiments/Labs: This is a form of discovery learning in science where students directly encounter the scientific process: making an observation, forming a hypothesis, testing the hypothesis, and coming to a conclusion. Teachers of ELLs need to make sure to preteach necessary content and functional vocabulary to enable full participation of English Language Learners.

Expert/Novice: This is a simulation involving two students. One student takes on the role of an expert and the other a novice in a particular situation. The expert responds to questions asked by the novice. The procedure can be used for lower level cognitive activities such as having students introduce one another to classroom procedures, and higher level activities such as explaining content area concepts at greater degrees of depth. The procedure can also be used to model the difference between formal and informal English, with the expert speaking formally and the novice informally. (Seidlitz & Perryman, 2008)

Field Notes: In this activity, students take notes and write reflections in a journals about what they are learning and experiencing. Field journals can be written or drawn and should be content focused, yet they can contain both social and academic language. (Samway, K., 2006)

Flash Card Review: To engage in this exercise, students make flash cards, preferably including images with explanations of the meanings of words. Students study, play games, and sort the flash cards in various ways.

Fluency Workshop: Students have three opportunities to talk and listen to another student about the same topic during this workshop. They alternate between listening and speaking. When listening, students may ask questions, but cannot contribute an opinion on the speaker's words. After the activity, students reflect on their level of fluency in the first and third discussion. (Maurice, K., 1983).

Formal/Informal Pairs: The teacher writes a statement on two strips of paper; one with formal English, one with informal English. The teacher distributes one strip to each student. Students have to find their match in the classroom. As an alternate activity, give pairs of strips to students. Have students match the pairs. This can be done individually or in small groups.

Four Corners Vocabulary: This is a way of processing vocabulary with a paper or note card divided into four sections: the term, a definition, a sentence, and an illustration. (Developed by D. Short, Center for Applied Linguistics. Described in:

Echevarria & Vogt, 2008)

Framed Oral Recap: This is an oral review involving two students using sentence starters. Students are given stems such as: "Today I realized...," "Now I know....," and "The most significant thing I learned was ...." Students pair up with a partner to discuss what they have learned in a lesson or unit. (Adapted from Zwiers, 2008)

Free Write: During free write, students write nonstop about a topic for five to ten minutes. The goal is to keep writing, even if they can't think of ideas. They may write "I don't know what to write" if they are unable to think of new ideas during the free write. English Language Learners can sketch and write in their native language although they should be encouraged to write in English. (Elbow, P. 1998) Writing with Power, Oxford University Press, 1981, 1998.

General Stems: These are incomplete sentences that scaffold the development of language structures to provide the opportunity for conversation and writing in any academic context.

Genre Analysis/Imitation: Students read high quality selections from a genre of literature during this activity. They note particular words, phrases, and ideas they found interesting or effective and record those in a journal. Students then use their notes and observations as a resource when writing in that genre. (Adapted from Samway, K., 2006)

Glossary Circles: Based on the idea of Literature Circles (Daniels, 1994)
In this activity, students work collaboratively on a set of related terms. They are given one glossary page per term, using a template that includes 4 squares labeled Vocabulary Enrichment, Illustration, Connections, and Discussion Questions. During learning, students share terms , illustrations, definitions, connections, and questions that have been added to the glossary page. (ie. study on polygons)

Graffiti Write: In small groups, students are asked to simultaneously list academic words tied to a particular concept, within a short time frame.

Graphic Organizers: Graphic organizers provide a way of developing a learner's schema by organizing information visually. Examples include the T-Chart,

Venn diagram, Concept Map, Concept Web, Timeline, etc. Graphic organizers are a form of nonlinguistic representation that can help students process and retain new information. (Marzano, R., Pickering., D. & Pollock., J., 2001)

Group Response with a White Board: Students write responses to questions on white boards using dry erase markers during this activity. These can be made from card stock slipped into report covers, or with shower board cut into squares that fit on student's desks. White boards are a form of active response signal shown to be highly effective in improving achievement for struggling learners.

Guided Notes: Teacher prepared notes used as a scaffold help students practice note-taking skills during lectures. For examples of guided note formats see:
http://www.studygs.net/guidednotes.htm

Hand Motions for Connecting Words: Gestures representing transition/signal words that students use to visually model the function of connecting words in a sentence. For example, students might bring their hands together for terms like: also, including, as well as, etc. For terms such as excluding, neither, without, no longer, etc., students could bring their hands together. Students can come up with their own signals for various categories including: comparing, contrasting, cause and effect, sequence, description, and emphasis. (Adapted from: Zwiers, 2008)

Hi-Lo Readers: Readers published on a variety of reading levels while having the same content focus and objectives. For example National Geographic Explorer Books can be found here:
http://new.ngsp.com/Products/SocialStudies/nbsp nbspNationalGeographicExplorerBooks/tabid/586/ Default.aspx And http://www.kidbiz3000.com/

Homophone/Homograph Sort: The teacher prepares homophone/homograph cards, listing words that sound the same, but are spelled differently, e.g., know/no, hear/here. The teacher asks the students to group the words that sound the same together and then explain the meanings of each.

IEPT (Inter-Ethnolingusitic Peer Tutoring): This is a research based method for increasing fluency in English Language Learners by pairing them with fluent English speakers. Tasks are highly structured and fluent English speakers are trained to promote more extensive interaction with English Language Learners (Johnson. D. 1995).

Idea Bookmarks: For this activity, students take reflective notes from the books they are reading on bookmark size pieces of paper. The bookmarks include quotes, observations, and words that strike the reader as interesting or effective. The bookmarks can be divided into boxes as quotes are added with page numbers written in each box. (Davies., K, 2006)

Improv Read Aloud: During this exercise, students act out a story silently that the teacher or another student reads aloud. Each student has a role and has to discover how to act out the story while it is being read. Afterward, students discuss how each student played their part during the improv. (Zwiers, 2008)

Insert Method: In this activity, students read text with a partner and mark the texts with the following coding system: a check to show a concept or fact already known, a question mark to show a concept that is confusing, an exclamation mark to show something new or surprising, or a plus to show an idea or concept that is new.
(Echevarria & Vogt, 2008)

Inside/Outside Circle: Students form two concentric circles facing one another, an inside circle and an outside circle. Students can then participate in short, guided discussion or review with their partner. After the discussion, the outside circle rotates one person to the right while the inside circle remains still. All students now have a new partner to speak with. This exercise facilitates student conversations. (Kagan, 1990)

Instructional Conversation: During this activity, students engage in conversation about literature through open- ended dialogue with the teacher or with students in small groups. Instructional conversations have few "known answer" questions and promote complex language and expression. (Goldenberg, C., 1992)

Instructional Scaffolding: This is model of teaching that helps students achieve increasing levels of independence following the pattern: teach, model, practice, and apply.(Echevarria, Vogt & Short, 2008)

Interactive Reading Logs: Reading logs are used by students during silent reading to reflect on the text. These logs can be exchanged with other students or with the teacher for questions , comments, or responses. These logs are ideal components of an SSR program.

Interview Grids: Interview grids help students record other student's responses to various questions. Students wander around the room and search for their partners who will respond to their questions. (Zwiers, 2008)

Keep, Delete, Substitute, Select: Students learn a strategy for summarizing developed by Brown, Campoine, and Day (1981) discussed in Classroom Instruction That Works (Marzano. R, Pickering D., & Pollock J., 2001) Students keep important information, delete unnecessary and redundant material, substitute general terms for specific terms (e.g. birds for robins, crows, etc.), and select or invent a topic sentence. For ELLs, Hill and Flynn (2006) recommend using gestures to represent each phase of the process and to explain the difference between high frequency and low frequency terms.

KID: Keyword, Information, Drawing In this activity, students list a word, important information about the word, and then a drawing of the word.

KIM Chart: A graphic organizer for students to organize what they are learning, have learned or for review. In the K section of the organizer students jot down key points that are being taught or that they have learned. In the I section students list important information that supports those points. And in the M section they come up with a visual representation that sums up the point and that will remind them of what was learned (Castillo ,2007)

KWL: This is a prereading strategy used to access prior knowledge and set up new learning experiences (Ogle, 1986). The teacher creates a chart where students respond to three questions: What do you know? What do you want to know? What have you learned? The first two questions are discussed prior to reading and the third is discussed afterward.

Language proficiency level: This is a measure of a student's ability to listen, speak, read, and write in English.

Learning Logs and Journals: Students can record observations and questions about what they are learning in a particular content area with learning logs or journals. The teacher can provide general or specific sentence starters to help students reflect on their learning.. (Samway, K., 2006)

Letters/Editorials: For this activity, students can write letters and editorials from their own point of view or from the point of view of a character in a novel, person from history, or a physical object (sun, atom, frog, etc.) Teachers of ELLs should remember to scaffold the writing process by providing sentence frames, graphic organizers, wordlists, and other writing supports. Newcomers may use the Draw/Write method discussed above.

Linguistic accommodations: The ways to provide access to curriculum and opportunities for language development for English Language Learners are: comprehensible input, differentiating based on language proficiency level, and scaffolding.

Literacy: To be literate, students have to have the ability to use and process printed and written material in a specific affective filter.

List Stressed Words: Students take a written paragraph and highlight words that would be stressed, focusing on stressing content English words such as nouns, verbs, adverbs over process words such as articles, prepositions, linking-verbs/modals and auxiliaries.

List/Group/Label: Students are given a list of words or students brainstorm a list of words as they engage in listing, grouping, and labeling. They sort the words on this list into similar piles and create labels for each pile. This can be done by topic (planets, stars, scientific laws, etc.) or by word type (those beginning with a particular letter, those with a particular suffix, those in a particular tense) (Taba, Hilda, 1967)

Literature Circles: In this activity students form small groups similar to "book clubs" to discuss literature. Roles include: discussion facilitators, passage pickers, illustrators, connectors, summarizers, vocabulary enrichers, travel tracers, investigators, and figurative language finders. ELLs will need to be supported with sentence starters, wordlists, and adapted text as necessary, depending on language level. (Schlick, N. & Johnson, N., 1999). For support in starting literature circles see: http://www.litcircles.org/ .

Margin Notes: This is a way of adapting text. Teachers, students, or volunteers write key terms, translations of key terms, or short native language summaries, text clarifications, or hints for understanding in the margins of a text book. (Echevarria, Vogt & Short, 2008)

Native Language Texts: Native language translations, chapter summaries, wordlists, glossaries, or related literature can be used to understand texts from content area classes. Many text book companies include Spanish language resources with the adoption.

Native Language Brainstorm: This method allows students to think about and list ideas related to a concept in their native language.

Nonlinguistic Representations: Nonverbal means of representing knowledge include illustrations, graphic organizers, physical models, and kinesthetic activities (Marzano, R., Pickering, D., & Pollock, J, 2001). Hill, J and Flynn, K. (2006) advocate integrating Total Physical Response (Asher J., 1967) as a means of integrating nonlinguistic representations because it engages learners in the early stages of language development.

Note Taking Strategies: Students learn strategies for organizing information presented in lectures and in texts during note-taking. English Language Learners, at the early stages of language development, benefit from guided notes (see above), native language wordlists, summaries, and opportunities to clarify concepts with peers. Strategies include informal outlines, concept webbing, Cornell Note taking, and combination notes. Research seems to indicate that students should write more rather than less when taking notes (Marzano, R., Pickering, D., and Pollock, J., 2001). ELLs in pre-production phases can respond to teacher notes through gesture. Those in early production and speech emergent phases can communicate about information in teacher prepared notes using teacher provided sentence frames. (Hill., J. & Flynn., K, 2006)

Numbered Heads Together: This strategy enables all students, in small groups, a chance to share with the whole class over time. Each student in a group is assigned a number (1, 2, 3 and 4). When asking questions the teacher will ask all the Ones to speak first, and then open the discussion to the rest of the class. For the next question, the teacher will ask the Twos to speak, then the Threes, and finally the Fours. The teacher can also randomize which number will speak in which order. When doing numbered heads with English Language Learners, teachers should provide sentence starters for the students. (Kagan, 1995).

Oral Scaffolding: This the process of:

• teaching academic language explicitly

• modeling academic language

• providing opportunities in structured ways for students to use language orally

• writing and using the language students have seen modeled and used in the classroom. (Adapted from Gibbons, 2002)

Outlines: This traditional note-taking method involves Roman numerals, Arabic numerals, and upper/lowercase letters.

Pairs View: This strategy keeps students engaged and focused while they process viewed material at a deeper level. When watching a video clip or movie, each pair of students is assigned a role. For example, one partner might be responsible for identifying key dates while another is listing for important people and their actions. (Kagan, S., 1992). Cooperative Learning. San Juan Capistrano, CA: Kagan Cooperative Learning.)

Paragraph Frames: Incomplete paragraphs are provided for students to scaffold the development of language structures that offer the opportunity for students to develop academic writing and communication skills.

Partner Reading: This strategy for processing text requires that two students read a text. Each can alternate a paragraph while the other summarizes or one can read and the other student summarize and ask questions. (Johnson, D., 1995)

Peer Editing: During this activity, students review one another's work using a rubric. Research shows that English Language Learners benefit from peer editing when trained using peer response strategies. (Berg, C., 1999)

Personal Dictionary: To engage in this activity, students choose words from the word wall, wordlists, or words encountered in texts. Words are recorded on note cards or in notebooks which become personal dictionaries. Students are encouraged to draw, reflect, or use their native language when defining the meaning of terms. (Adapted from Echevarria, Vogt, & Short, 2008)

Personal Spelling Guide: In this activity, students record correct spellings of misspelled words on note cards. As the number of cards grows, students sort the words, based on each word's characteristics. Students should generate the categories. For example, students may develop lists like: contractions, big words, words with "ie" or "ei", words that are hard to say, words I never used. Encourage students to look for patterns in the spellings of the words as they make lists. To assess their knowledge of spelling words, students can select a number of words to review and have a partner quiz them orally their self-selected words.

Perspective-Based Writing: This activity requires students to write from an assigned point of view using specific academic language. For example, students in a social studies class could write from the perspective of Martin Luther King , Jr., to explain his participation in the Montgomery bus boycott to a fellow pastor. Students should be given specific words and phrases to integrate into the writing assignment. Students can also write from the point of view of inanimate objects such as rocks, water, molecules, etc. and describe processes from an imaginative perspective. In addition, students can take on the role of an expert within a field: math, science, social studies, or literature, and use the language of the discipline to write about a particular topic. Genre studies can be particularly helpful as a way of preparing students for perspective-based writing activities. (Seidlitz & Perryman, 2008).

Posted Phrases and Stems: Sentence frames posted in clearly visible locations in the classroom to enable students to have easy access to functional language during a task. For example, during a lab the teacher might post the stems: How do I record...., Can you help me (gather, mix, measure, identify, list...., Can you explain what you mean by ...? Frames should be posted in English but can be written in the native language as well.

Prediction Café: This activity is a way to have students participate in mini-discussions about prediction. Pick out important headings, quotes, or captions from a text (about eight quotes for a class of 24). Students discuss what they think the text is about or what they think will happen in the text. (Note: Even though some students may receive the same card, predictions will vary.) Students should be given frames to facilitate the development of academic language during the activity such as: __makes me think that.., I believe ___ because..., etc.). (Zwiers, J., 2008)

Pretest with a partner: Students are given a pretest, in pairs. Students take turns reading the questions. After each question they try to come to consensus , and then they record an answer. (Echevarria, J. & Vogt. M., 2008)

QtA (Question the Author): This is a strategy for deepening the level of thinking about literature (Beck,. I. & McKeown, M., Hamilton, R., & Kugan. L., 1997). Instead of staying within the realm of the text, the teacher prompts the students to think about the author's purpose. For example:

• What do you think the author is trying to say?

• Why do you think the author chose that word or phrase?

• Would you have chosen a different word or phrase?

Question Answer Relationship (QAR): This is a way of teaching students to analyze the nature of questions they are asked about a text. Questions are divided into four categories (Echevarria J., & Vogt M., 2008)

• Right there (found in the text)

• Think and Search (requires thinking about relationships between ideas in the text)

• Author and Me (requires making an inference about the text)

• On My Own (requires reflection on experience and knowledge)

Question, Signal, Stem, Share, Assess: This is a strategy to get students to use new academic language during student-student interactions. The teacher asks a question and then asks students to show a signal when they are ready to respond to the question, using a particular sentence stem provided by the teacher. Students share their answers. Students are then assessed orally or in writing

(Seidlitz, J., & Perryman B., 2008).

Quick Write: Within a short time period, students are asked to respond in writing to a specific content concept.

Radio Talk Show: Students create a radio talk show about a particular topic. This can be a good opportunity for students to practice using academic language as they take on the role of an expert. It can also provide an opportunity for students to identify the distinctions between formal and informal use of English as they play different roles. (Wilhelm., J., 2002)

R.A.F.T.: This social studies writing strategy enables students to write from various points of view (Fisher, D. & Frey, N., 2004). The letters stand for Role (the perspective the students take, Audience (the individuals the author is addressing), Format (the type of writing that will take place), Topic (the subject).

Read, Write, Pair, Share: This strategy encourages students to share their writing and ideas during interactions. Students read a text, write their thoughts using a sentence starter, pair up with another student, and share their writing. Students can also be given suggestions about responding to one another's writing. (Fisher, D. & Frey, N., 2007).

Reader/Writer/Speaker Response Triads: This is a way of processing text in cooperative groups. Students form groups of three. One student reads the text aloud; one writes the group's reactions or responses to questions about the text, a third reports the answers to the group. After reporting to the group, the students switch roles. (Echevarria J., & Vogt M., 2007)

Recasting: For this activity, repeat an English Language Learner's incorrect statement or question correctly. Do not chang the meaning or the low risk environment Be sure the learner feels comfortable during the interaction. Recasts have been shown to have a positive impact on second language acquisition (Leeman, J., 2003).

Reciprocal Teaching: This is a student-student interaction involving collaboration to create meaning from texts (Palincsar & Brown, 1985). Hill and Flynn (2006) suggest adapting reciprocal teaching for use among English Language Learners

by providing vocabulary, modeling language use, and using pictorial representation during the discussion. Reciprocal teaching involves a student leader who guides the class through stages: Summarizing, Question Generating, Clarifying, and Predicting.

Related Literature: These are texts connected to and supportive of text used in class content areas. These texts can be fiction or nonfiction, in the native language, or in the target language. (Echevarria, J., & Vogt, M., Short. D., 2008)

ReQuest: This is a variation of reciprocal teaching (see above). The teacher asks questions using particular stems following a period of SSR. After another period of SSR, the teacher provides stems for students to use when responding to text.. (Manzo, A., 1969: as cited in Fisher, D. & Frey, N., 2007)

Retelling: Students can retell a narrative text in their own words or summarize an expository text in their own words when they engage in this activity.

Same Scene Twice: Students perform a skit that involves individuals discussing a topic. The first time, the individuals are novices who use informal language to discuss the topic. The second time, they are experts who discuss the topic using correct academic terminology and academic English. (adapted from Wilhelm, J., 2002)

Scanning: Students scan through a text backwards looking for unfamiliar terms. The teacher then provides quick, brief definitions for the terms, giving only the meaning of the word as it appears in context. Marzano, Pickering, and Pollock (2001) state that "even superficial instruction on words greatly enhances the probability that students will learn the words from context when they encounter them in their reading and that, "the effects of vocabulary instruction are even more powerful when the words selected are those that students most likely will encounter when they learn new content."

Segmental Practice: Listening/Discrimination activities that help learners listen for and practice pronouncing individual combinations of syllables. There are several ways to engage in segmental practice. Tongue twisters and comparisons with native language pronunciations can help English

Language Learners practice English pronunciation. The activity "syllable, storm, say" involves students brainstorming syllables that begin with a particular sound for example: pat, pen, pal, pas, pon, pen, etc. Long and short vowel sounds can be used as well as diphthongs. Students then practice in partners pronouncing the terms. (Celce-Murcia, M., Brinton. D. & Goodwin. J, 1996).

Self-Assessment of Levels of Word Knowledge:
Students rank their knowledge of new words on the word wall and other word lists using total response signals (see below) or sentence starters. Responses range from no familiarity with the word to understanding a word well enough to explain it to others. (Diamond & Gutlohn, 2006: as cited in Echevarria, Vogt, Short, 2008)

Sentence frames: Incomplete sentences are provided for students to scaffold the development of language structures that provide the opportunity for students to develop academic language.

Sentence Mark Up: Students use colored pencils to mark texts for cause and effect, opposing thoughts, connecting words, and other features of sentences. This helps students understand the relationship between clauses. (Zwiers, J., 2008)

Sentence Sort: This activity requires students to sort various sentences based on characteristics. The teacher provides the sentences and students sort them. This can be done with an open sort where students create the categories or a closed sort where the teacher creates the categories. It can also be done by taking a paragraph from a textbook or from class literature. Possible categories include:
• Description sentences
• Complex sentences
• Simple sentences
• Sentences connecting ideas
• Sentences comparing ideas
• Sentences opposing ideas
• Sentences with correct usage
• Sentences with incorrect usage
• Sentences in formal English
• Sentences in informal English

Sentence Stems: Incomplete sentences are provided for students to scaffold the development of specific language structures and to facilitate entry into conversation and writing. For example "In my opinion..." or "One characteristic of annelids is...

Signal Words: Signal words determine a text pattern such as generalization, cause and effect, process, sequence, etc. A sample of signal words can be found at:
www.nifl.gov/readingprofiles/Signal_Words.pdf

Six Step Vocabulary Process: This research based process, developed by Marzano (2004) helps teachers employ methods develop academic vocabulary. The steps are: Teacher provides a description. Students restate the explanation in their own words. Students create a nonlinguistic representation of the term. Students periodically do activities that help them add to their knowledge of vocabulary terms. Periodically students are asked to discuss the terms with each other. Periodically, students are involved in games that allow them to "play" with the terms.

Sound Scripting: This is a way for students to mark text showing pauses and stress. Students use a writing program to write a paragraph, enter a paragraph break to show pauses, and use capital and bold letters to show word stress. (Powell, M., 1996)

SQP2RS (Squeepers): This classroom reading strategy trains students to use cognitive/metacognitive strategies to process nonfiction text. The following steps are involved (Echevarria, Vogt, Short, 2008):

• Survey: students scan the visuals, headings, and other text features.

• Question: students write a list of questions they might find answers to while reading

• Predict: student write predictions about what they will learn

• Read: students read the text

• Respond: students revisit their questions and think through responses to reading

SSR Program (Sustained, Silent Reading): This program encourages students to read books of their choice during a silent reading period of 15-20 minutes per day. Pilgreen (2000) discusses eight features of high quality SSR programs: access to books, book appeal, conducive reading environment, encouragement to read, non-accountability, distributed reading time, staff training, and follow up activities. (Pilgreen, 2000).

Story Telling: In this activity, students retell narratives in their native language.

Structured Academic Controversy: This is a way of structuring classroom discussion to promote deep thinking and to understand multiple perspectives. Johnson & Johnson (1995) outline five steps.

• Organizing Information And Deriving Conclusions

• Presenting And Advocating Positions

• Uncertainty Created By Being Challenged By Opposing Views

• Epistemic Curiosity And Perspective Taking

• Reconceptualizing, Synthesizing, and Integrating

Structured Conversation: In this activity, student/student interaction is explicitly planned. Students are given sentence frames to begin the conversation as well as specific questions and sentence starters for the purpose of elaboration.

Summarization Frames: This is a way of structuring summaries of content area text. The frames involve specific questions that help students summarize different kinds of texts. Marzano (2001 p. 27-42) and Flynn & Hill (2006) discuss seven frames:

• narrative frame
• topic restriction frame
• illustration frame
• definition frame;
• argumentation frame;
• problem solution frame
• conversation frame

Suprasegmental Practice: This pronunciation practice involves units and groups of syllables. Some techniques include: sound scripting (see above), recasting (see above), a pronunciation portfolio, and content/function word comparisons. (Wennerstrom, A., 1993).

Systematic Phonics Instruction: This activity teaches sound-spelling relationships and how to use those relationships when reading. The national literacy panel (Francis, D.J., Lesaux, N.K., & August, D.L., 2006) reported that instruction in phonemic awareness, phonics, and fluency had "clear benefits for language minority students."

Taped Text: Recordings of text can be used as a way of adapting text for English Language Learners. (Echevarria, Vogt, & Short, 2008)

Think Alouds: Thinking aloud allows teachers to scaffold cognitive and metacognitive thinking by verbalizing the thought process. (Bauman, Jones, & Seifert-Kessell, 1993)

Think, Pair, Share: This method encourages student-student interaction. The teacher asks a question and then provides wait time. The students then find a partner and compare their answers. Afterward, selected students share their thoughts with the whole class. (Lyman, 1981)

Ticket Out: For this activity, students write a short reflection at the end of a lesson. Teachers can ask students to reflect on what they have learned. As students write they can use new vocabulary learned during the lesson.

Tiered Questions: In this activity, a varying types of questions to students, based on their level of language development. (Hill & Flynn, 2006)

Tiered Response Stems: this activity, ask a single question, but allow students to choose from a variety of stems to construct responses. Students can choose a stem based on their level of language knowledge and proficiency. (Seidlitz & Perryman, 2008)

Total Physical Response (TPR): This is a way of teaching that uses gesture and movement to make content comprehensible to ESL newcomers. (Asher, J., 1967)

Total Response Signals (Also called active response signals): Active responses such as thumbs up/down, white boards, and response cards can be used by students. Response signals enable teachers to check for understanding instantly, and students can self-assess current levels of understanding.

Unit Study for ELLs: This is a modified approach to writers workshop advocated by Samway (2006). The steps involve:

• Teachers gather high quality samples of the genre

• Teachers provide time for immersion in books

• Sifting between books that students can model and those that they can't

• Students immerse themselves a second time in the books

• Students try the "writing moves" used by accomplished writers

- Students write and publish
- Students reflect and assess

Visual Literacy Frames: This is a framework for improving visual literacy focusing on affective, compositional, and critical dimensions of visual information processing. (Callow, J., 2008).

Visuals: Illustrations, graphic organizers, manipulatives, models, and real world objects are used to make content comprehensible for English Language Learners.

Vocabulary Game Shows: Using games like Jeopardy, Pictionary, and Who Wants to be a Millionaire etc., allows students a chance to practice academic vocabulary.

Vocabulary Self-Collection: This ia a research-based method of vocabulary instruction involving student collection of words for class study. Students share where the word was found, the definition, and why the class should study that particular word. (Ruddell, M., & Shearer, B., 2002)

W.I.T. Questioning: This is a questioning strategy that trains students to use three stems to promote elaboration in discussion (Seiditz & Perryman, 2008):
- Why do you think...?
- Is there another...?
- Tell me more about...

Whip Around: This is a way of getting input from all students during a class discussion. The teacher asks students to write a bulleted list in response to an open- ended question. Students write their responses to the question and then stand up. The teacher then calls on students, one at a time, to respond to the question. If students have the same answer they mark it off on their papers. The teacher continues to call on students, and students continue to mark their answers. When all their answers have been marked, the students sit down. The activity continues until all students are seated. (Fisher, D. & Frey, N., 2007)

Word Analysis: In this activity, students study the parts, origins, and structures of words for the purpose of improving spelling (Harrington, 1996).

Word Generation: In this activity, students

brainstorm words having particular roots. Teachers then have students predict the meaning of the word based on the roots. (Echevarria, Vogt & Short, 2008)

Word MES Questioning: This is a method of differentiating instruction for ELLs developed by Hill & Flynn (2006). The mnemonic device stands for "Word, Model, Expand, and Sound." Teachers work on word selection with pre-production students. "Model for early production. Expand what speech emergence students have said or written and help intermediate and advanced fluency students sound like a book" by working on fluency.

Word Play: In this activity, students manipulate words through various word games to increase understanding. Johnson, von Hoff Johnson, & Shlicting (2004) divide word games into eight categories: onomastics (name games), expressions, figures of speech, word associations, word formations, word manipulations, word games, and ambiguities.

Word Sorts: Sorting words based on structure and spelling can improve orthography (Bear, D. & Invernizzi, M., 2004).

Word Splash: Identify what you want students to know about a certain concept (key vocabulary or words connected to the concept). Write the words randomly and in all directions. Tell students you wrote the words in no particular order (called a splash). After presenting the lesson have students begin to place the words in some logical order and use the words in either speaking or writing.

Word Study Books: In this activity, students organize words in a notebook based on spelling, affixes and roots. (Bear D., & Invernizzi, M., 2004).

Word Walls: This is a collection of words posted on a classroom wall. Word walls are organized by topic, sound, or spelling and help improve literacy. (Eyraud et al., 2000)

Written Conversation: Using planned language and content, students interact during writing conversation. In pairs, students respond to one another's specific questions and sentence starter.

This page is intentionally left blank.

Bibliography

Asher, J. and Price, B. "The Learning Strategy of Total Physical Response: Some Age Differences." *Child Development*, 38, 1219-1227. 1967.

Asher, J. "The Total Physical Response Approach to Second Language Learning." *The Modern Language Journal* (53) 1. 1969.

August, D. and Shanahan, T. "Developing Literacy in Second Language Learners: Report of the National Literacy Panel on Language-Minority Children and Youth." *Center for Applied Linguistics*, Lawrence Erlbaum Associates: Mahwah, NJ. 2006.

Ausubel, D. P. "The Use of Advance Organizers in the Learning and Retention of Meaningful Verbal Material." *Journal of Educational Psychology*, 51, 267-272. 1960.

Baker, L. "Reading Comprehension and Science Inquiry: Metacognitive Connections." In E.W.Saul (Ed.), "Crossing Borders in Literacy and Science Instruction: Perspectives on Theory and Practice." Newark, DE: *International Reading Association*; Arlington, VA: *National Science Teachers Association* (NSTA) Press. 2004.

Bauman, J. F., Russell, N. S., and Jones, L. A. "Effects of Think-aloud Instruction on Elementary Students' Comprehension Abilities. *Journal of Reading Behavior*, 24 (2), 143-172. 1992.

Bear, D.R., Invernizzi, M., Templeton, S., & Johnson, F. *Words their Way: Word Study for Phonics, Vocabulary, and Spelling Instruction (2nd Ed.).* Upper Saddle River, NJ: Merrill Prentice Hall. 2004.

Beck, I.L., McKeown, M.G., Hamilton, R.L., & Kugan, L. "Questioning the Author: An Approach for Enhancing Student Engagement with Text." Newark, DE: International Reading Association. 1997.

Berg, C. "The Effects of Trained Peer Response on ESL Students' Revision Types and Writing Quality." *Journal of Second Language Writing,* Volume 8, Issue 3, 215-241. September 1999,

Boulware, B.J., & Crow, M. "Using the Concept Attainment Strategy to Enhance Reading Comprehension." *The Reading Teacher, 61*(6), 491–495. March, 2008.

Brown, A., Campoine, J., and Day, J. "Learning to Learn: On Training Students to Learn from Texts." *Educational Researcher, 10,* 14-24. 1981.

Bruner, J., Goodnow, J. & Austin, G. A. *A Study of Thinking.* New York: Science Editions. 1967.

Chamot, A.U. & O'Malley, *J.M. The Calla Handbook: Implementing the Cognitive Academic Language Learning Approach.* White Plains, NY: Addison Wesley Longman. 1994.

Callow, J. Show Me: "Principles for Assessing Students' Visual Literacy." *The Reading Teacher, 61*(8), 616–626. May, 2008.

Celce-Murcia, M., Brinton, D. & Goodwin, J. *Teaching Pronunciation: A Reference for Teachers of English to Speakers of Other Languages.* Cambridge: Cambridge University Press. 1996.

Cunningham-Flores, M. *Improving Adult ESL Learners' Pronunciation Skills.* National Center for ESL Literacy Education. 1998.

Dole, J., Duffy, G., Roehler, L., & Pearson, P. "Moving from the Old to the New: Research in Reading Comprehension Instruction." *Review of Educational Research, 61,* 239-264. 1991.

Echevarria, J., Short, D & Vogt, M. *Making Content Comprehensible. The Sheltered Instruction Observation Protocol.* Boston, MA: Pearson. 2008.

Elbow, P. *Writing with Power.* Oxford: Oxford University Press. 1998.

Eyraud, K., Giles, G., Koenig, S., & Stoller, F. "The Word Wall Approach: Promoting L2 Vocabulary Learning". *English Teaching Forum*, 38, 2-11. 2000.

Fisher, D., & Frey, N. *Checking for Understanding: Formative Assessment Techniques for your Classroom.* Alexandria, VA: Association for Supervision and Curriculum Development. 2007.

Francis, D., Lesaux, N., & August, D. "Language of Instruction for Language Minority Learners." In D. L. August & T. Shanahan (Eds.) *Developing Literacy in a Second Language: Report of the National Literacy Panel.* (pp.365-414). Mahwah, NJ: Lawrence Erlbaum Associates. 2006.

Gibbons, P. *Scaffolding Language, Scaffolding Learning.* Portsmouth, NH: Heinemann. 2002.

Goldenberg, C., "Instructional Conversations: Promoting Comprehension through Discussion, *The Reading Teacher, 46 (4)*, 316-326. 1992-1993.

Harrington, M. J. "Basic Instruction in Word Analysis Skills to Improve Spelling Competence." *Education*, 117, 22. Available: http://www.questia.com/ 1996.

Head, M., & Readence, J. "Anticipation Guides: Meaning through Prediction." In E. Dishner, T. Bean, J. Readence, & D. Moore (Eds.), *Reading in the Content Areas,* Dubuque, IA: Kendall/Hunt. 1986.

High, Julie. *Second Language Learning through Cooperative Learning.* San Clemente, CA: Kagan Publishing. 1993.

Hill, J., & Flynn, K. *Classroom Instruction that Works with English Language Learners.* Alexandria, VA: Association for Supervision and Curriculum Development. 2006.

Johnson, D., & Johnson, R. *Creative Controversy: Intellectual Challenge in the Classroom* (3rd ed.). Edina, MN: Interaction Book Company. 1995.

Kagan, S. *Cooperative learning for students limited in language proficiency.* in M. Brubacher, R. Payne & K. Rickett (Eds.), *Perspectives on Small Group Learning.* Oakville, Ontario, Canada. 1990.

Kagan, S. *Cooperative Learning.* San Juan Capistrano, CA: Kagan Cooperative Learning. 1992.

Kirschner, P., Sweller, J., & Clark, R. "Why Minimal Guidance during Instruction Does Not Work: An Analysis of the Failure of Constructivist, Discovery, Problem-based, Experiential, and Inquiry-based Teaching". *Educational Psychologist* 41 (2): 75–86. 2006.

Krashen, S. *Principles and Practices in Second Language Acquisition.* Oxford: Pergamon. 1982.

Leeman, J. Recasts and Second Language Development: Beyond Negative Evidence. *Studies in Second Language Acquisition, 25,* 37-63. 2003.

Lyman, F. T. "The Responsive Classroom Discussion: The Inclusion of All Students." In A. Anderson (Ed.), *Mainstreaming Digest* (pp. 109-113). College Park: University of Maryland Press. 1981.

Marzano, R. *Building Academic Background.* Alexandria, VA: MCREL, ASCD. 2004.

Marzano, R., Pickering, D. J., & Pollock, J. E. *Classroom Instruction that Works.* Alexandria, VA: MCREL, ASCD. 2001.

Maurice, K. "The Fluency Workshop." *TESOL Newsletter,* 17, 4. 1983.

Mayer, R. *Learning and Instruction.* New Jersey: Pearson Education, Inc. 2003.

"Principles and Standards for School Mathematics." *National Council of Teachers of Mathematics* NCTM. Reston, VA: NCTM. 2000.

Novak, J.D. "Concept Mapping: A Strategy for Organizing Knowledge." in Glynn, S.M. & Duit, R. (eds.), *Learning Science in the Schools: Research Reforming Practice,* Lawrence Erlbaum Associates, Mahwah, NJ. 1995.

Ogle, D. S. "K-W-L Group Instructional Strategy." In A. S. Palincsar, D. S. Ogle, B. F. Jones, & E. G. Carr (Eds.), *Teaching Reading as Thinking* (Teleconference Resource Guide, pp. 11-17). Alexandria, VA: Association for Supervision and Curriculum Development. 1986.

Palincsar, A.S., & Brown, A.L. "Reciprocal Teaching: Activities to Promote Reading with Your Mind." In T.L. Harris & E.J. Cooper (Eds.), *Reading, Thinking and Concept Development: Strategies for the Classroom*. New York: The College Board. 1985.

Paulk, W. *How to Study in College*. Boston: Houghton Mifflin, 2000.

Pilgreen, J. *The SSR Handbook: How to Organize and Maintain a Sustained Silent Reading Program*. Portsmouth, NH: Heinemann. 2000.

Pilgreen, J. and Krashen, S. "Sustained Silent Reading with English as a Second Language with High School Students: Impact on Reading Comprehension, Reading Frequency, and Reading Enjoyment." *School Library Media Quarterly* 22: 21-23. 1993.

Powell, M. *Presenting in English*. Hove: Language Teaching Publications. 1996.

Chamot, A., & O'Malley, J. "The Calla Handbook: Implementing the Cognitive Academic Language Learning Approach." *Reading,* MA: Addison-Wesley 1994.

Ruddell, M.R., & Shearer, B.A. "'Extraordinary,' 'tremendous,' 'exhilarating,' 'magnificent': Middle school At-Risk Students Become Avid Word Learners with the Vocabulary Self-Collection Strategy (VSS). *Journal of Adolescent and Adult Literacy, 45*(4), 352-363. 2002.

Samway, K. *When English Language Learners Write: Connecting Research to Practice.* Portsmouth: Heineman. 2006.

Schlick Noe, K. & Johnson, N. *Getting Started with Literature Circles*. Norwood, MA: Christopher-Gordon Publishers, Inc. 1999.

Seidlitz, J. & Perryman, B. *Seven Steps to Building an Interactive Classroom: Engaging All Students in Academic Conversation.* San Clemente, CA: Canter Press. 2008.

Taba, H. *Curriculum Development: Theory and Practice*. New York: Harcourt Brace & World. 1962.

Taba, Hilda. *Teachers' Handbook for Elementary Social Studies*. Reading, MA: Addison-Wesley. 1967.

Taylor, W. "Cloze Procedure, A New Tool for Measuring Readability." *Journalism Quarterly.* 30, 415-433. 1953.

Thornburry, S. *How to Teach Speaking.* Essex, England: Pearson. 2005.

Vail, Neil J. and Papenfuss, J. *Daily Oral Language Plus.* Evanston, IL: McDougal, Littell. 1993.

Weaver, C. *Teaching Grammar in Context*. Portsmouth, NH: Boynton, Cook Publishers. 1996.

Wennerstrom, A. "Content-Based Pronunciation." *TESOL Journal*, 1(3), 15-18. 1993.

White, T., Sowell, J., & Yanagihara, A. "Teaching Elementary Students to Use Word-Part Clues." *The Reading Teacher, 42*, 302-308. 1989.

Willhelm., J *Action Strategies for Deepening Comprehension.* New York: Scholastic. 2002.

Zwiers, J. *Building Academic Language.* Newark, DE: Jossey-Bass/International Reading Association. 2008.

Three ways to order {

- **FAX** completed order form with payment information to **(949) 200-4384**
- **PHONE** order information to **(210) 315-7119**
- **ORDER ONLINE** at **www.seidlitzeducation.com**

Pricing, specifications, and availability subject to change without notice.

PRODUCT	PRICE	QTY	TOTAL$
NEW! ¡Toma la Palabra!	$32.95		
NEW! Pathways to Greatness for Secondary ELL Newcomers	$32.95		
NEW! Teaching Social Studies to ELLs	$24.95		
NEW! Boosting Achievement: Reaching Students with Interrupted or Minimal Education	$26.95		
NEW! ELLs in Texas: What Teachers Need to Know 2ND EDITION	$34.95		
ELLs in Texas: What Administrators Need to Know 2ND EDITION	$29.95		
NEW! Talk Read Talk Write: A Practical Routine for Learning in All Content Areas K-12 2ND EDITION	$32.95		
Vocabulary Now! 44 Strategies All Teachers Can Use	$29.95		
Diverse Learner Flip Book	$26.95		
ELPS Flip Book	$19.95		
Academic Language Cards and Activity Booklet, ENGLISH	$19.95		
Academic Language Cards, SPANISH	$9.95		
Sheltered Instruction Plus	$19.95		
RTI for ELLs Fold-Out	$16.95		
7 Steps to a Language-Rich Interactive Classroom	$29.95		
7 Pasos para crear un aula interactiva y rica en lenguaje SPANISH	$29.95		
	COLUMN 1 TOTAL $		

PRODUCT	PRICE	QTY	TOTAL$
38 Great Academic Language Builders	$24.95		
Navigating the ELPS: Using the Standards to Improve Instruction for English Learners	$24.95		
Navigating the ELPS: Math (2nd Edition)	$24.95		
Navigating the ELPS: Science	$24.95		
Navigating the ELPS: Social Studies	$29.95		
Navigating the ELPS: Language Arts and Reading	$34.95		
'Instead Of I Don't Know' Poster, 24" x 36" ☐ Elementary ENGLISH ☐ Secondary ENGLISH	$9.95		
'Instead Of I Don't Know' Poster, 24" x 36" SPANISH (Elementary only)	$9.95		
'Please Speak In Complete Sentences' Poster 24" x 36" ☐ ENGLISH ☐ SPANISH	$9.95		
20 pack 'Instead Of I Don't Know' Posters, 11" x 17" ☐ Elementary ENGLISH ☐ Secondary ENGLISH	$40.00		
20 pack 'Instead Of I Don't Know' Posters, 11" x 17" SPANISH (Elementary only)	$40.00		
20 pack 'Please Speak In Complete Sentences' Posters, 11" x 17" ☐ ENGLISH ☐ SPANISH	$40.00		
	COLUMN 2 TOTAL $		

COLUMN 1+2	$	
DISCOUNT	$	
SHIPPING	$	
TAX	$	
TOTAL	**$**	

SHIPPING 9% of order total, minimum $14.95
5-7 business days to ship. If needed sooner please call for rates.
TAX EXEMPT? please fax a copy of your certificate along with order.

NAME

SHIPPING ADDRESS   CITY   STATE, ZIP

PHONE NUMBER   EMAIL ADDRESS

TO ORDER BY FAX
to **(949)200-4384**
please complete
credit card info **or**
attach purchase order

☐ **Visa**   ☐ **MasterCard**   ☐ **Discover**   ☐ **AMEX**

CARD #   EXPIRES
                         mm/yyyy
SIGNATURE   CVV
                         3- or 4- digit code

☐ **Purchase Order attached**
please make P.O. out to **Seidlitz Education**

For information about Seidlitz Education products and professional development, please contact us at

(210) 315-7119 | kathy@johnseidlitz.com
56 Via Regalo, San Clemente, CA 92673
www.seidlitzeducation.com

Giving kids the gift of **academic language.**™

Seidlitz EDUCATION

REV126717

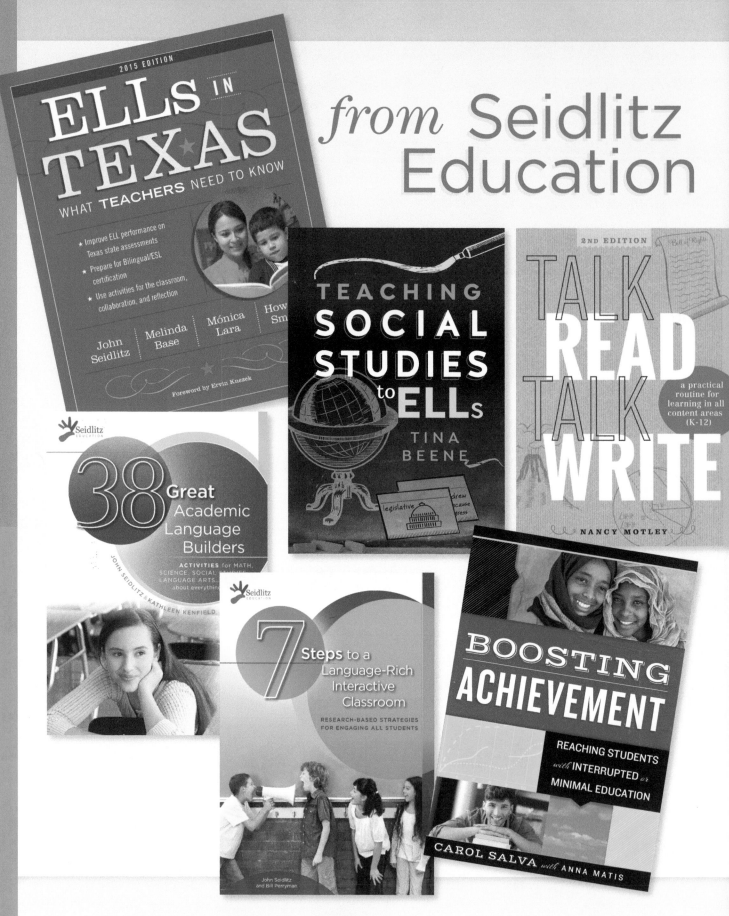